AF243826

Parish Asceticism

James Lloyd Breck Conference on Monasticism and the Church
2021

Edited by Greg Peters

Contributions by
Luigi Gioia
Alexis Torrance

Nashotah House Press

Nashotah House Theological Seminary
2777 Mission Road
Nashotah, WI 53058

Religion

ISBN-13 978-0-9792243-7-9

Parish Asceticism

JAMES LLOYD BRECK CONFERENCE
ON
MONASTICISM AND THE CHURCH
2021

Edited by
Greg Peters

Acknowledgments

The Breck Conference would not be possible without the support of Dr. Garwood Anderson, Dean, and the residential faculty of Nashotah House.

The staff of Nashotah House, especially Labin Duke, Laura Groetsch, and Randy Savage.

Dawn Anderson and the Rev. Ben Jefferies helped prepare the talks for publication.

Without the generous endowment of the Order of St. Benedict Servants of Christ, there would be no James Lloyd Breck Conference on Monasticism and the Church.

Introduction

The James Lloyd Breck Conference on Monasticism and the Church is made possible by a generous endowment granted to Nashotah House Theological Seminary in 2017, extending the legacy of the Order of St. Benedict Servants of Christ into perpetuity for the advancement of Religious Life, especially within Anglicanism. Founded in 1968 by the Very Rev. Dom Cornelis deRijk, OSB (along with the Rev. Canon Lewis Long), in Phoenix, Arizona, the Order was a Benedictine community guided by the balance of prayer, study, and work. Rev. deRijk, the last prior of the Order, received his Master of Divinity degree from Nashotah House in 1976. With his passing in 2016 the Order closed, but its end allows for a new beginning with the creation of the annual Breck Conference.

The conference name was chosen to honor one of the founders of Nashotah House while also being clear that the conference was on monasticism but with the purpose of recovering elements of the Christian monastic tradition for the contemporary church. James Lloyd Breck, while a student at General Theological Seminary in New York, responded to an invitation by Bp. Jackson Kemper to come to the Wisconsin frontier. In correspondence with his brother, Breck wrote, "The following is mooted [i.e., spoken] in our class–and be not surprised if time should strengthen it–that six or eight of us clan together, going out West, place ourselves under Bishop Kemper, all at one point, and there educate and preach; to live under one roof, constituted into a Religious House, under a Superior."[1] Simply put, Breck imagined that what was to become Nashotah House was a monastic endeavor.[2]

The theme of the second conference, held on the campus of Nashotah House from June 24-25, 2021, was "Parish Asceticism." The Christian tradition takes for granted that baptized believers will engage in some form of bodily training for the purpose of godliness (cf. 1 Tim. 4:7-8). The Apostle Paul said, "I always take pains to have a clear conscience toward God and toward men" (Acts 24:16). That is, he engaged in asceticism for the purpose of being in relationship with God and with all humankind, motivated certainly by Jesus' admonition to "love the Lord your God with all your heart and with all your soul and with all your mind. This is the great and first commandment. And a second is like it: You shall love your neighbor as yourself. On these two commandments depend all the Law and the Prophets" (Matt. 22:37-40). Moreover, the "phenomenon

---

[1] James Lloyd Breck, June 15, 1840 letter to his brother Charles; cited in *The Life of the Reverend James Lloyd Breck, D.D., chiefly from Letters Written by Himself*, compiled by Charles Breck (New York: E. & J. B. Young & Co., 1883), 8.

[2] Thomas C. Reeves, "James Lloyd Breck and the Founding of Nashotah House," *Anglican and Episcopal History* 65.1 (1996), 56: "James Lloyd Breck was the most zealous member of the quartet, and the one most interested in monasticism."

of asceticism is indeed a subject of perennial and universal interest" (John Behr).

Oftentimes, however, the language of "asceticism" conjures images of emaciated monks and nuns who fled to the desert to engage in a kind of harsh asceticism that today would appear to be rooted more in psychological disorder than the love of God. But such an understanding is distorted and a caricature of good and proper Christian asceticism. Thus, the 2021 Breck Conference explored the main elements of Christian monasticism to present its varied and rich history, attempting to recover this tradition as an essential element in today's Church, and not only for monks but for all baptized Christians. For it is in the crucible of the parish where all Christians become ascetics.

The conference consisted of four plenary talks by two speakers and included much time for informal discussion and interaction. The speakers included

Rev. Dr. Luigi Gioia (Associate Priest at St Paul's Church, Knightsbridge, London, and Research Associate of the Von Hügel Institute, St. Edmund's College in the University of Cambridge)

Rev. Dr. Alexis Torrance (Archbishop Demetrios Associate Professor of Byzantine Theology at the University of Notre Dame)

Abbreviations

PG   *Patrologiae cursus completus: Series Graeca*, ed. J.
        P. Migne, 161 vols. Paris: Migne, 1857-1866.

RB   *Rule of Benedict*

SC   *Sources Chrétiennes*. Paris: Cerf, 1942-.

ed. Kambylis   Athanasios Kambylis, ed., *Symeon Neos
        Theologos: Hymnen*. Berlin/New York:
        De Gruyter, 1976.

Early Western Christian Asceticism and the Rule of St. Benedict: Passions, Bodies, and Love

Rev. Dr. Luigi Gioia

"It is well known that there are four kind of monks."[3]

By the beginning of the sixth century, when Benedict of Nursia (d. 547) wrote this sentence, the Christian ascetic tradition had been familiar with monasticism for almost a century and a half, especially since Athanasius of Alexandria (d. 373) had written his *Life of Antony* (d. 356) around the year 365, which had been translated into Latin by Evagrius of Antioch shortly afterwards, in 374 (an anonymous Latin translation had already been in circulation before then). Anthony might not have been literally the first monk, but, especially in the West, the influence of his biography on the birth and growth of monastic tradition cannot be overstated.

Significant in this regard is the testimony of Augustine of Hippo (d. 430), who chanced upon the *Life of Antony*

---

[3] RB 1.1.

soon after it was translated, in 386,[4] and attributes to it a role in his conversion. Antony's decision to embrace a stricter form of ascetic life upon hearing a passage from Matthew's Gospel read in church[5] leads Augustine to interpret the children's chant "Pick up and read" as a summons to open his Bible and read the passage from Romans which won him over to faith once for all.[6] Later Augustine reveals that, like Antony, he had "meditated taking flight to live in solitude."[7] On becoming a Christian, he too embraced ascetical life, and wrote a rule for monks and nuns and several ascetical treatises, of which I shall say more later.

Benedict writes his Rule during a period that spans from the 520s until his death in 547. By that time, the West had known a prodigious flowering of monastic forms of life and he could rely on a considerable body of monastic writings, chief among them the works of John Cassian (d. 435), who had become the main conveyer of the Eastern ascetical tradition to the West, making available in the Latin language the teaching of the first Egyptian monks, the so-called Fathers of the Desert, and especially of one of the most influential Greek theoreticians of the spiritual life, Evagrius Ponticus (d. 399).[8]

---

[4] Augustine of Hippo, *Confessions* 8.6.15.

[5] Athanasius of Alexandria, *Life of Antony* 2.

[6] Augustine of Hippo, *Confessions* 8.12.29.

[7] Augustine of Hippo, *Confessions* 10.43.70; Henry Chadwick, trans., *Saint Augustine: Confessions* (Oxford: Oxford University Press, 1991), 220.

[8] Scholars disagree on whether Cassian depended directly on Evagrius or not. In any case, the similarity in several aspects of their teaching are

So RB's review of the different kind of monks follows the same taxonomy established by Jerome[9] and Cassian,[10] which, rather than a description, works as a rhetorical expedient aimed at emphasizing principles of ascetical life which had become consolidated in the West because they were considered safer. This means that by stigmatizing monks called "sarabaites" and "gyrovagues," the RB expresses the conviction that it is not possible to lead a serious ascetical life without referring to authority and experience combined with stability in the same community. The real focus of the chapter, however, is on the two forms of monastic life which had become traditional in both East and West, namely solitary life (usually designated as eremitic or anchoretic) and life in a community (usually designated as cenobitic).

The crucial role played by the *Life of Antony* in the spreading of the monastic ideal in the West gave the impression that life as a hermit not only had been the first to appear chronologically, but also was the highest and most perfect form of asceticism. Was not this implied by what seems the most obvious etymology of the word "monk," namely she or he who is *monos*, "alone"; that is, "she or he who leads a solitary life"? Athanasius' account of the ascetical endeavor of the first monk establishes a

---

undeniable and even if this depends on them having had the same masters, the key thing for us is that Cassian was the conveyer of this tradition to the West.

[9] Jerome, *Ep* 22.34.

[10] John Cassian, *Conferences* 18.4-8.

pattern that became normative in monastic hagiography: a person first withdraws to the desert or wilderness, there she is tested and tempted during several decades of solitary life, and once she has won the battle against the devil (that is, achieved perfection), she is qualified to teach others to do the same, and therefore God starts sending disciples to her. According to this model, life in common appears not so much because it has an intrinsic ascetical value but as a means for disciples to learn from a master, as in a school.

So when Gregory the Great (d. 604) wrote his biography of St. Benedict, he adopted this by then well-established hagiographical pattern: Benedict withdraws to Subiaco and lives there alone in a cave for a number of years, and once he has won the battle against the devil and the flesh, he becomes a master for the many disciples who come to learn from him, to be at his "school." This also is the model implied by the Prologue of Benedict's Rule in which a master speaks to an individual disciple and exhorts him to embrace a form of ascetical life based on obedience and in which the monastery or community is described as a "'school," that is a place where the reason for living together is learning from an experienced teacher:

> Listen carefully, my son, to the master's instructions, and attend to them with the ear of your heart. This is advice from a father who loves you; welcome it, and faithfully put it into practice. The labor of obedience will bring you back to him from whom you had drifted through the sloth of disobedience. This message of mine is for you, then, if you are ready to give up your own will, once and for all, and

armed with the strong and noble weapons of obedience to do battle for the true King, Christ the Lord. . . , Therefore we intend to establish a school for the Lord's service.[11]

The chapter on the different kinds of monks that immediately follows the Prologue, however, while paying lip-service to this individual and ascensional model, in fact subtly disrupts it in several ways.

First of all, it starts not with hermits but with "coenobites," that is those who embrace a committed and stable form of life in common: "First, there are the cenobites, that is to say, those who belong to a monastery, where they serve under a rule and an abbot."[12] Eremitic life is listed in the second place and described in ways which undermine the traditional narrative concerning its chronological and ascetical priority. For RB, this is a form of life which some people might be able to adopt only after they have lived with others for a long time because life in a community is the only context in which their ability and intentions can be tested safely and authentically:

> Second, there are the anchorites or hermits, who have come through the test (*probatio*) of living in a monastery for a long time, and have passed beyond the first fervor of monastic life. Thanks to the help (*solacium*) and guidance of many, they are now trained (*iam docti*) to fight against the devil. They have built up their strength (*extructi*) and go from the battle line in the ranks of their brothers to the

---

[11] RB Prol 1-3, 45; Timothy Fry, ed., *RB 1980: The Rule of St. Benedict* (Collegeville, MN: Liturgical Press, 1981), 157, 165.

[12] RB 1.2; Fry, ed., *RB 1980*, 169.

single combat of the desert. Self-reliant (*sufficiunt*) now, without the support (*consolatio*) of another, they are ready (*securi*) with God's help to grapple single-handed with the vices of body and [of the thoughts] (*contra vitia carnis vel cogitationum*).[13]

What is striking in this passage is the praise of life in common which offers *probatio, solacium,* and *consolatio,* that is (i) verified methods of discernment and guidance, and (ii) something which is very weakly conveyed by the English translation of "help" and "support." *Solacium* and *consolatio* mean "soothing, assuaging, comfort, relief" and the RB as a whole makes clear that these are not just virtues useful to achieve some further and more important objective, but are values in themselves, because they capture something of the essence of what Christian life is about.[14]

Apparently, therefore, this section offers a flattering description of hermits, and yet in the light of the monastic ideal portrayed by the RB as a whole, it sounds more like a warning against forms of solitary ascetical endeavor. Hermits are *iam docti, extructi, securi,* that is, "already experts," "well equipped," or "able to rely on themselves alone." Ironically, Benedict does add *Deo auxiliante,* "with God's help," to these qualities, but the cleverly constructed Latin sentence ends with what, in evangelical terms, sounds more like a fatal blow: *sufficiunt,* that is "they are above the need for others in their lives."

---

[13] RB 1.3-5.

[14] John 14.

This insinuates much more than a simple caution concerning a form of ascetical life which might be admirable but is too challenging for the average monk (in fact, Benedict shows a predilection for the average monk). Here Benedict is in fact distancing himself from the tradition he inherits from Cassian and Evagrius Ponticus. This tradition is suggested when RB says that the hermit is qualified to fight not only against the devil, but especially *contra vitia carnis vel cogitationum*, "against the vices of the flesh and of the thoughts." Mention of the "thoughts" is a veiled reference to Evagrius' theory of eight principal "thoughts" which was transmitted to the West as the eight principal vices and became eventually better known as the seven capital sins.[15] Benedict had become familiar with it through the teaching of Cassian's fifth conference: "There are eight principal vices which attack humankind. The first gluttony, which means the voraciousness of the belly; the second is fornication; the third is filargyria, which is avarice or love of money; the fourth is anger; the fifth is sadness; the sixth is acedia, which is anxiety or weariness of heart; the seventh is cenodoxia, which is boastfulness or vainglory; and the eighth is pride."[16]

At stake here is not just whether monks should live alone or in common, but the entire approach to what qualifies as an authentically Christian form of ascetical life

---

[15] Fry, ed., *RB 1980*, 344.

[16] John Cassian, *Conferences* 5.12; Boniface Ramsey, trans., *John Cassian: The Conferences* (New York: Paulist Pres, 1997), 183.

from a theological point of view and especially one question which can broadly be defined as the issue of moral elitism and which is at the heart not only of asceticism and spiritual life, but also of the life of the church.

One of the passages of RB where the influence of Cassian, and through him of Evagrius, is more clearly recognizable is in chapter seven, "On humility," which is the longest chapter of the RB and amounts to a miniature treatise of spirituality. It compares progress in ascetical endeavor to the climbing of a ladder (this is what we meant earlier by the "ascensional" model) in which each step represents a practice or a virtue which the monastic needs to cultivate if she wants to "reach the highest summit" (*culmen*):

> if we want to reach the highest summit (*culmen*) of humility . . . then by our ascending actions we must set up that ladder. . . . Now the ladder erected is our life on earth, and if we humble our hearts the Lord will raise it to heaven. We may call our body and soul the sides of this ladder, into which our divine vocation has fitted the various steps of humility and discipline as we ascend.[17]

There is no clear progression from one step to the other, except the traditional overall transition from the fear of God, which is the first step, to love, which is presented as the outcome of this process. This chapter of RB reproduces almost literally Cassian's fourth conference and espouses the approach to the dynamics of spiritual life which Cassian shares with Evagrius. According to this model,

---

[17] RB 7.5-6, 8-9; Fry, ed., *RB 1980*, 193.

there are two clearly distinguishable stages in spiritual life: the practical life and the contemplative life, which are so subordinated one to the other that it is impossible to attain to the latter without passing through the former: "The first kind is πρακτική, or practical, which reaches its fulfillment in correction of behaviour [*sic*] and in cleansing from vice. The other is θεωρητική, which consists in the contemplation of divine things and in the understanding of most sacred meanings."[18] Let us leave aside contemplative life for the moment, and focus on the "practical life" because this is what is described both by Cassian's fourth conference and by the seventh chapter of RB, namely the attainment of a level of purification from vices and an acquisition of virtues such that it enables the monastic to act virtuously spontaneously, freely, not out of fear, but out of love. According to Cassian

> this practical perfection exists in a twofold form. Its first mode is that of knowing the nature of all the vices and the method of remedying them. The second is that of discerning the sequence of the virtues and forming our mind by their perfection in such a way that it is obedient to them not as if it were coerced and subjected to an arbitrary rule but as taking pleasure in and enjoying what is so to say a natural good, thus mounting with delight the hard and narrow way.[19]

---

[18] John Cassian, *Conferences* 14.1.2; Ramsey, trans., *John Cassian: The Conferences*, 505.

[19] John Cassian, *Conferences* 14.3.1; Ramsey, trans., *John Cassian: The Conferences*, 506.

And indeed at the end of his fourth institute, Cassian states that

> When [humility] is possessed in truth, it will at once bring you a step higher to love, which has no fear. Then all the things that you used to do out of a certain dread of punishment you will begin to do without any difficulty, as it were naturally, and no longer with a view to punishment or fear of any kind, but out of love for the good itself and out of pleasure in virtue.[20]

The influence of this passage is clearly recognizable in the conclusion of Benedict's chapter on humility:

> Now, therefore, after ascending all these steps of humility, the monk will quickly arrive at that *perfect love* of God which *casts out fear* (1 John 4:18). Through this love, all that he once performed with dread, he will now begin to observe without effort, as though naturally, from habit, no longer out of fear of hell, but out of love for Christ, good habit and delight in virtue. All this the Lord will by the Holy Spirit graciously manifest in his workman now cleansed of vices and sins.[21]

The goal of the practical life for Evagrius was *apatheia*, "impassibility" or "passionlessness," a state that he thought he had attained, according to Palladius.[22] Evagrius seems to have believed that "although temptations do not cease, the soul could achieve a God-given state in which it becomes

---

[20] John Cassian, *Institutes* 4.39; Boniface Ramsey, trans., *John Cassian: The Institutes* (New York: Newman Press, 2000), 100.

[21] RB 7.67-70; Fry, ed., *RB 1980*, 202-203. Cf. the end of the Prologue and of Chapter 73 which convey the same message.

[22] Palladius, *Lausiac History* 38.

impervious to evil."[23] The reason monastics should strive to achieve apatheia through the practical life is that it gives access to love: "divine charity possesses you as a result of *apatheia*."[24]

While subscribing to the same idea, Cassian prefers not to use the language of *apatheia* which had become suspicious in some Christian circles because of its Stoic connotations,[25] and instead states that the end of the practical life is "purity of heart," which corresponds to charity.

> For the sake of this, then, everything is to be done and desired. For its sake solitude is to be pursued; for its sake we know that we must undertake fasts, vigils, labors, bodily deprivation, readings, and other virtuous things, so that by them we may be able to acquire and keep a heart untouched by any harmful passion, and so that by taking these steps we may be able to ascend to the perfection of love.
>
> These observances do not exist for themselves. If perchance we are unable to carry out some strict obligation of ours because we are prevented by some good and necessary business, we should not fall into sadness or anger or indignation, which we would have intended to drive out by doing what we omitted. For what is gained by fasting is less than what is spent on anger, and the fruit that is obtained from reading is not so great as the loss that is incurred by contempt for one's brother. It behooves us, then, to carry out the things that are secondary–namely, fasts, vigils, the solitary life, and meditation on Scripture–for the sake of the principle scopos [i.e., goal], which is purity of heart or love.[26]

---

[23] Fry, ed., *RB 1980*, 39.

[24] Evagrius Ponticus, Ep. 61, cited in Fry, ed., *RB 1980*, 361.

[25] Cf. the harsh criticism by Jerome, Ep. 133, for example.

[26] John Cassian, *Conferences* 1.7.1-2; Ramsey, trans., *John Cassian: The*

According to some commentators, this demonstrates that the object of RB was

> only to expose the first part of the 'spiritual science,' *praktikè*... St. Benedict intends to lead the monk to the end of this practical way, to *apathéia* (once his worker has been cleansed of vices and sins), to the perfection of virtues (effortlessly; as if spontaneously, good habit itself and a delight in virtue) and to charity (the monk will soon arrive at that perfect love of God that drives out fear; no longer out of fear of hell, but out of love for Christ)... St. Benedict limited himself to the first part of the program, referring his student to the second part to the classics of oriental monastic spirituality. But the very terms of RB 73 show that for him this *perfectio conversationis*, this *celsitudo perfectionis*, is the normal outcome of a fervent monastic life.[27]

In a nutshell, RB as a whole intends to lead the monastics to the end of the practical life and allow them to acquire the "purity of heart" (or the *apatheia*, "passionlessness") which then gives access to love – a love understood as (i) ease in the practice of virtue and (ii) the means to embark on the second stage, namely the contemplative life, that is, a deeper and experiential knowledge of God, and possibly some form of mystical experience.

Indeed, this seems to find a confirmation in the last chapter of RB (Chapter 73 – Not the Whole Observance of Righteousness Is Laid Down in this Rule):

Conferences, 45-46.

[27] Placide Deseilles, "Concerning the Epilogue to RB 7," *American Benedictine Review* 58 (2007), 277-279.

The reason we have written this rule is that, by observing it in monasteries, we can show that we have some degree of virtue and the beginnings of monastic life. But for anyone hastening on to the perfection (*perfectio*) of monastic life, there are the teachings of the holy Fathers, the observance of which will lead him to the very heights of perfection (*celsitudo perfectionis*). What page, what passage of the inspired books of the Old and New Testaments is not the truest of guides for human life? What book of the holy catholic Fathers does not resoundingly summon us along the true way to reach the Creator? Then, besides the *Conferences* of the Fathers, their *Institutes* and their *Lives*, there is also the rule of our holy father Basil. For observant and obedient monks, all these are nothing less than tools for the cultivation of virtues; but as for us, they make us blush for shame at being so slothful, so unobservant, so negligent. Are you hastening toward your heavenly home? Then with Christ's help, keep this little rule that we have written for beginners. After that, you can set out for the loftier summits (*culmina*) of the teaching and virtues we mentioned above, and under God's protection you will reach them. Amen.[28]

A more careful reading, however, shows that on the contrary again here Benedict is distancing himself from what we have called the "individual and ascensional" ascetical model, in ways similar to those we detected earlier in Chapter one – On the different kinds of monks.

In Chapter 73 he does refer to those who hasten "on to the perfection of monastic life," want to reach the "very heights of perfection" and directs them to the reading of Scripture, to "the *Conferences* of the Fathers, their *Institutes*

---

[28] RB 73.1-9; Fry, ed., *RB 1980*, 295-297.

and their *Lives*," that is the writings of Cassian, and to "the rule of our holy father Basil." With regards to the monastic project codified in his rule, however, he is happy to say that "the reason we have written this rule is that, by observing it in monasteries, we can show that we have some degree of virtue and the beginnings of monastic life" and to add that it is "a little rule written for beginners," that is for people who "blush for shame at being so slothful, so unobservant, so negligent."

This is not rhetorical feigned humility. A constant feature of RB is the care for the little ones, those who struggle, those who are average. He is not interested in the strong but in the weak, as we shall see. Our point is, therefore, that there seems to be a tension in RB between the "individual and ascensional" model and a deeply engrained and instinctive wariness against any ascetical practice that smacks of moral and spiritual elitism. One of the ways of unearthing this tension is teasing out the two main sources of the RB. So far, we have focused on what Benedict owes to Cassian (and through him to the Eastern ascetical tradition); we now turn our attention to what he owes to the other great Western early ascetical authority, namely Augustine of Hippo.

Augustine's Monastic Teaching

We have seen the role Athanasius' *Life of Antony* played in Augustine's conversion and in his decision to embrace ascetical life. Augustine lived in a community during the time between his return to Africa in 388 and his episcopal ordination some ten years later, and he is the author of a brief rule, the *Regula ad Servos Dei*, written perhaps about 397 for the monastery at Hippo,[29] and of a number of ascetical treatises, letters, and sermons.[30] When compared with Cassian's emphasis on the relationship of each individual to God and on discipleship to a master (i.e., the monastery seen more as a "school"), the most striking feature of Augustine's teaching is his assiduous and totalizing focus on the relationships of monastics to one another and on the theological significance of the community.[31]

For Augustine, community love is so essential to the monastic ideal that he bends the etymology of the word *monachus* to accommodate this interpretation:

> Why then should we not use the term "monks" when the psalm says, *See how good and how pleasant it is for*

---

[29] See George P. Lawless, *Augustine of Hippo and his Monastic Rule* (Oxford: Oxford University Press, 1987) and Luc Verheijen, *La Règle de saint Augustin*, 2 vols. (Paris: Études augustiniennes, 1967).

[30] The *De opere monachorum*, the *De sancta virginitate*, the letters 210 and 211, the *Sermons* 355 and 356, and the *Exposition on Psalm* 132.

[31] Mutual love in a community of course was very important for the tradition represented by Cassian and Evagrius too. Cassian in particular considers the Christian community of Jerusalem described in Acts 4.32-35 as the ideal monastic community (Conf 18.5). However, as we have seen, both Evagrius and Cassian tend to present love or charity as the result of an initial work or purification of vices and growth in virtues (the practical life) and as the presupposition for the following stage of 'theoretical life,' that is, the knowledge of God. This is the pattern we have seen at work in RB's chapter on humility.

brothers to dwell together in unity? Μόνος means "one," but not any kind of "one." One person may be present in a crowd; he is "one," but one with many others. He can be called "one" but not μόνος, because μόνος means "one alone." But where people live together in such unity that they form a single individual, where it is true of them, as scripture says, that they have but *one mind and one heart* (Acts 4:32)—many bodies but not many minds, many bodies but not many hearts—then they are rightly called μόνος, "one alone."[32]

Monastics are so called not because they live alone or choose a celibate form of life (which incidentally is the most reliable etymology of the word "monk" from an historical point of view[33]) but because they are of one mind and one heart with one another. This is the idea presented in the opening sentence of Augustine's rule:

> The chief motivation for your sharing life together is to live harmoniously in the house and to have one heart and one soul seeking God. Do not call anything your own; possess everything in common. Your superior ought to provide each of you with food and clothing, not on an equal basis to all, because all do not enjoy the same health, but to each one in proportion to his need. For you read in the Acts of the Apostles: "They possessed everything in common," and "Distribution was made to each in proportion of each one's need."[34]

---

[32] Augustine of Hippo, *Exposition of Psalm* 132.6; Maria Boulding, trans., *Expositions of the Psalms (Enarrationes in Psalmos) 121-150* (Hyde Park, NY: New City Press, 2004), 181.

[33] Cf. Fry, ed., *RB 1980*, 301-321 on the history of the word "monk."

[34] Augustine of Hippo, *Regula ad Servos Dei* 1.2-3; Lawless, *Augustine of Hippo and his Monastic Rule*, 81. Cf. Fry, ed., *RB 1980*, 63: "While the life

For Augustine, love is both the starting point and the aim of life in common because God is love. This theme is pervasive in his theology but nowhere it is expressed more lyrically that in his *Commentary on the First Letter to St. John* and in his *Sermons on John's Gospel*. In one of the most revealing formulations of this view he says, "love your neighbour and look upon the source in you from which you love your neighbour; there you will see, as far as you can, God."[35]

The Augustinian Wave

Augustine's works enjoyed a wide popularity already during his lifetime, but curiously the influence of his teaching on Western monastic authors can be detected only much later, almost a century after his death. From that

---

of Augustine's monastery is dominated by the demands of fraternal charity, the observances themselves are the traditional monastic practices: humility, psalmody, private prayer, *lectio*, fasting, silence, simplicity of food and clothing, obedience, manual labor, renunciation of property, strict chastity. In general, the regime is quite mild compared to Egyptian austerity, though Augustine can be severe in matters of principle, such as private property and unsuitable relationships with women. The monks slept in individual cells, but meals were taken in common to the accompaniment of table reading. The majority of the African monks were ex-slaves or at least from the poorer classes. Communities were presided over by a *presbyter*, probably a priest appointed by the bishop, and a *praepositus*, who was second in command. If the basic observances were the same as in the East or in Europe, there was nevertheless a difference of tone in the monasticism of Augustine."

[35] Augustine of Hippo, *Tractate on the Gospel of John* 17.8; John W. Rettig, trans., *St. Augustine: Tractates on the Gospel of John 11–27* (Washington, DC: Catholic University of America Press, 1988), 116.

moment onward, however, it had an impact comparable to the sudden opening of a dam, and its omnipresence in monastic literature led scholars to describe it as the "Augustinian wave."[36]

Especially relevant for our topic is the fact that the first clear instance of this "wave" can be found in 525 in the writings of Caesarius of Arles (d. 542), who was going to play an important role in the so-called "semi-Pelagian" controversy, as we shall see. Almost at the same time, in 530, in Naples (that is, very close to Benedict's monastery of Montecasino), the abbot Eugippius (d. 535) includes Augustine's rule in a florilegium. Benedict had started to write his rule around the year 520, mainly under the influence of Cassian (through his main source, the *Regula Magistri*), but kept revising it until his death in 547. This explains why the Augustinian influence is detectable—especially in the last part of the RB, which is the section he wrote after the Augustinian wave reached him, around the year 530.

Augustinian Influences on RB

The first time that concern for fraternal relations clearly comes to the fore in RB is with the chapter dedicated to the cellarer; that is, the monastic in charge of provisioning

---

[36] Fry, ed., *RB 1980*, 64. The expression is that of Adalbert de Vogüé in "Saint Benoît et son temps: Règles italiennes et règles provençales au VI e siècle" *Regula Benedicti Studia* 1 (1972): 169-193; see also his "The Cenobitic Rules of the West" *Cistercian Studies* 12 (1977): 175-183.

and catering. There is something of a division of tasks in a Benedictine monastery: the abbot should be more concerned with the spiritual leadership whereas the cellarer looks after the practical aspects of the life of the community, which is a field where incompetence and negligence can be highly disruptive. This is why great care is devoted to the choice of the right monastic for this role:

> As cellarer of the monastery, there should be chosen from the community someone who is wise, mature in conduct, temperate, not an excessive eater, not proud, excitable, offensive, dilatory or wasteful, but God-fearing, and like a father to the whole community. He will take care of everything, but will do nothing without an order from the abbot.[37]

Considering how pivotal this role is in a Benedictine monastery, it is significant to see quotations from Augustine's works appear for the first time in this chapter. Thus, the injunction that "If any brother happens to make an unreasonable demand of him," the cellarer "should not reject him with disdain and cause him distress, but reasonably and humbly deny the improper request,"[38] and then that he should "be humble. If goods are not available to meet a request, he will offer a kind word in reply,"[39] contain echos of a sentence from Augustine's exposition of Psalm

---

[37] RB 31.1-5; Fry, ed., *RB 1980*, 227.

[38] RB 31.7; Fry, ed., *RB 1980*, 229.

[39] RB 31.13; Fry, ed., *RB 1980*, 229.

103.[40] A similar care for harmony in fraternal relations appears in the prescription that the cellarer should "provide the brothers their allotted amount of food without any pride or delay, lest they be led astray. For he must remember what the Scripture says that person deserves *who leads one of the little ones astray* (Matt 18:6),"[41] a sentence inspired by one of Augustine's letters.[42] In this same chapter we also find the first parallel to the rule of Augustine in the prescription that "Necessary items are to be requested and given at the proper times, so that no one may be disquieted or distressed in the house of God."[43]

When Augustine, at the beginning of his rule, describes the foundations of monastic life, one of the key injunctions concerns the necessity to give up any private property, share everything in common and make sure that monastics receive what they need not equally but according to their needs:

> Here are the rules we lay down for your observance, once you have been admitted to the monastery. The chief motivation for your sharing together is to live harmoniously in the house and to have one heart and one soul seeking God. Do not call anything your own; possess everything in common. Your superior ought to provide each of you with

---

[40] Augustine of Hippo, *Exposition of Psalm* 103.19

[41] RB 31.16; Fry, ed., *RB 1980*,

[42] Augustine of Hippo, Ep 22.6.

[43] RB 31.18-19; Fry, ed., *RB 1980*, 229, which echoes Augustine of Hippo, *Regula ad Servos Dei* 5.10: "Books are to be requested at a definite hour each day; requests made at other times will be denied" (Lawless, *Augustine of Hippo and his Monastic Rule*, 97).

food and clothing, not on an equal basis to all, because all do not enjoy the same health, but to each one in proportion to his need. For you read in the Acts of the Apostles: 'They possessed everything in common', and 'Distribution was made to each in proportion to each one's need.' Those who owned anything in the world should freely consent to possess everything in common in the monastery.[44]

This same teaching is detailed in two chapters of Benedict's rule, Chapter 33 (On Whether Monks Ought to Have Anything of Their Own) and Chapter 34 (On Whether All Should Receive in Equal Measure What Is Necessary). Then, two more quotations from Augustine's rule concern grumbling and praying: monastics should serve each other without grumbling,[45] and they should take care not to disturb those who wish to keep praying personally and silently in the chapel between offices.[46]

It might be argued that while concerning key aspects of life in common, the quotations enumerated so far do not alter the overall ascetical model Benedict inherits from Cassian and Evagrius. Indeed, Augustine's influence alters

---

[44] Augustine of Hippo, *Regula ad Servos Dei* 1.1-5; Lawless, *Augustine of Hippo and his Monastic Rule*, 81.

[45] RB 35.13, quoting Augustine of Hippo, *Regula ad Servos Dei* 5.9: "Those responsible for food, clothing, or book are to serve their brothers without grumbling" (Lawless, *Augustine of Hippo and his Monastic Rule*, 97).

[46] RB 52.1-2, quoting Augustine of Hippo, *Regula ad Servos Dei* 2.2: "No one has any business in the prayer-room apart from the particular purpose which it serves; that is why it is called the oratory. Consequently, if some wish to pray even outside the scheduled periods, during their free time, they should not be deterred by people who think they have some other task there" (Lawless, *Augustine of Hippo and his Monastic Rule*, 85).

the RB's ascetical framework substantially only in the last section, especially in the chapters in which Benedict revisits some of the themes he had dealt with in the first part of the Rule but this time from a distinctly Augustinian viewpoint: namely, in the chapters devoted to the role of the abbot, fraternal relations, and obedience.

We have seen how one of the main features of the monastic model which Benedict inherits from Cassian is the priority given to the relation of each individual monk to the master or abbot. Thus, in the first part of the Rule, the chapter devoted to the abbot focusses on his duties and responsibility, on his teaching, and presents him as occupying the "place of Christ in the monastery."[47] When Benedict reassesses the role of the abbot in Chapter 64, we find in it three of the most distinctive quotations from Augustine in the whole RB, namely that the abbot "must hate faults but love the brothers,"[48] that he should "recognize that his goal must be profit for the monks, not pre-eminence for himself,"[49] and that he should "strive to be loved rather than feared."[50] Beyond the significance of these quotations, however, it is striking to see how the role of the community suddenly becomes much more prominent: the abbot should be elected by "the whole community acting unanimously

---

[47] RB 2.2; Fry, ed., *RB 1980*, 173.

[48] RB 64.11; Fry, ed., *RB 1980*, 283, quoting Augustine of Hippo, *Regula ad Servos Dei* 4.10; *Sermon* 49.5; and *The City of God* 14.6.

[49] RB 64.8; Fry, ed., *RB 1980*, 283, quoting Augustine of Hippo, *Regula ad Servos Dei* 7.3: *Sermon* 340.3; and the *City of God* 19.19.

[50] RB 64.15; Fry, ed., *RB 1980*, 283, quoting Augustine of Hippo, Ep 211.15.

in the fear of God, or by some part of the community, no matter how small, which possesses sounder judgment."[51]

The reversal of Cassian's ascetic model, however, appears with the greatest clarity in what is unanimously considered to be the most mature expression of Benedictine spirituality, namely the short and incisive Chapter 72 (The Good Zeal of Monks). There is only one direct quotation from Augustine's rule in this chapter, but the underlying theology of the passage is unmistakably Augustinian through and through. Whereas in the model inspired by Cassian, which we saw at work in RB 7 (On Humility), love is the result of the purification from vices and of the acquisition of virtues, in Chapter 72 love (called here "good zeal") is the starting point:

> Just as there is a wicked zeal of bitterness which separates from God and leads to hell, so there is a good zeal which separates from evil and leads to God and everlasting life. This, then, is the good zeal which monks must foster with fervent love.[52]

Augustine expresses the same idea in a well-known sentence from the *Confessions*: "My weight is my love. Wherever I am carried, my love is carrying me."[53] In other words, love is the starting point of ascetic endeavor (notice how it is the good zeal that separates from evil) and pulls

---

[51] RB 64.1-2; Fry, ed., *RB 1980*, 281.

[52] RB 72.1-3; Fry, ed., *RB 1980*, 295.

[53] Augustine of Hippo, *Confessions* 13.9.10; Chadwick, trans., *Saint Augustine: Confessions*, 278.

the monastic in a given direction. Monastic life consists in leaving behind the "wicked zeal which separates from God" and embracing a good zeal "with fervent love." For Benedict as for Augustine, in the spiritual life there is no neutral point, we never reach a rest or, for that matter, any "perfection." If we do not keep moving towards God, thanks to love, we are inevitably pulled further and further away from him, not necessarily by choosing evil but simply by inertia. Here is how Augustine describes this principle in the *Confessions*:

> To whom can I expound, and with what words can I express, the weight of cupidity pulling us downwards into the precipitous abyss and the lifting up of love given by your Spirit who was 'borne above the waters'?... This symbolic language [of the book of Genesis] contains a resemblance, but also a difference. It means our feelings and our loves. The impurity of our spirit flows downwards because of our love of anxieties, and the holiness which is yours draws us upwards in a love of freedom from anxiety.[54]

Then there is another striking difference between the end of Chapter seven on humility and Chapter 72. Chapter seven talked about reaching a *"perfect love of God which casts out fear* (1 John 4:18)" and enables the monastic "to observe without effort, as though naturally, from habit, no longer out of fear of hell, but out of love for Christ, good habit and delight in virtue"[55] – which is a rather abstract

---

[54] Augustine of Hippo, *Confessions* 13.7.8; Chadwick, trans., *Saint Augustine: Confessions*, 277.

[55] RB 7.67-69; Fry, ed., *RB 1980*, 201-203.

description of love. In Chapter 72, love is not about purification from vices and acquisition of virtues, nor part of a wider quest for perfection, but is described entirely with reference to interpersonal relations:

> [Monastics] *should each try to be the first to show respect to the other* (Rom 12:10), supporting with the greatest patience one another's weaknesses of body or behavior, and earnestly competing in obedience to one another. No one is to pursue what he judges better for himself, but instead, what he judges better for someone else. To their fellow monks they show the pure love of brothers; to God, loving fear; to their abbot, unfeigned and humble love. Let them prefer nothing whatever to Christ, and may he bring us all together (*omnes pariter*) to everlasting life.[56]

The individualistic model of search for perfection at the school of a master in which life in common tended to be seen as a means to exercise one's virtues is replaced by the determination to aim at eternal life "all together," *omnes pariter*. An image will help to visualize this shift: the model inspired by Cassian can be compared to a marathon where everyone tries to win, and in principle everyone can win, by doing what is required to reach the finish line. In the model inspired by Augustine, the best runners slow down to encourage, support, and carry the weakest runners, and victory consists in reaching the finish line together, *omnes pariter*. Monastics know that they can rely on their sisters' and brothers' "greatest patience" because everyone has "weaknesses of body or behavior." One of the main traits

---

[56] RB 72.4-12; Fry, ed., *RB 1980*, 295.

of RB is its insistence on the weakness, the failings, the limitations of the monks "of this generation" and the need to exercise extreme moderation and "arrange everything in such a way that the strong have something to yearn for and the weak nothing to run from."[57]

Moral Elitism
and the So-called 'semi-Pelagian' Controversy

In what we have seen so far in this theological overview of early Western asceticism, our purpose has not been that of opposing Cassian to Augustine nor of attributing to RB a final option in favour of the latter over the former. As far as Benedict is concerned, had he wanted to opt exclusively for an Augustinian ascetical model over against the model represented by Cassian and Evagrius, he could have re-written the whole rule – after all, there was a gap of over fifteen years between the moment Benedict was reached by the "Augustinian wave" and his death. On the contrary, Benedict seems to have been happy to combine the two models in his rule and leave whatever tension might arise between them unresolved. He considered that such tension would have allowed his monks to benefit from both traditions. With the light of almost two centuries of experience of monastic asceticism, we see that Benedict seems to have understood that the Eastern and especially the Egyptian tradition inherited through Cassian could be

---

[57] RB 64.19; Fry, ed., *RB 1980*, 283.

fruitful only on one condition: neutralize its potential for moral elitism, which increasingly had been perceived as a threat by all serious practitioners of monasticism.

In a nutshell, this is the issue at stake: monastics take some distance not only from the "world" but also from the ecclesial community; moreover, they embrace a discipline of life which requires an extra effort[58] with the hope of achieving something that is often described in terms of "perfection."[59] How to pre-empt the possibility that the practitioners of this discipline see themselves as better or more virtuous than those who do not embrace it? And even more so, how to prevent the temptation to perceive this discipline as a feat ultimately dependent on willpower?

These are not abstract questions. It is not an accident if Pelagianism, in its many forms and resurgences, has tended to thrive in monastic circles – Pelagius himself was a monk.

The Pelagian controversy occupied Augustine during the last twenty years of his life, from 411 to the year of his death in 430. It resurfaced again during Benedict's lifetime in a bout misleadingly known under the name of "semi-Pelagianism." Interestingly, two of the figures more often quoted in relation to semi-Pelagianism are characters we have become familiar with: Cassian and Caesarius of Arles. Moreover, the resolution of this controversy happened with the Council of Orange, in 529, which is exactly when Benedict was writing his rule.

---

[58] Cf. RB Prol.

[59] Cf. RB 1 and 73.

I will not attempt here to summarize the whole question surrounding this controversy but only point out few aspects which are relevant for the present paper and especially the question of moral elitism. First of all, none of the actors in this controversy talks about "semi-Pelagianism." The term was introduced only during the dispute on grace in the sixteenth century[60] and it is highly misleading when applied to the debates on this issue in the fifth and sixth centuries. It is true however that in his Conference 13, Cassian unwisely waded into this highly sensitive debate and exposed himself to the censorious zeal of Prosper of Aquitaine (d. 455), a litigious self-appointed paladin of Augustinian orthodoxy in southern Gaul. The anti-Pelagianism of Cassian is not in question, but it is undoubtable that he shared the disquiet of a number of monastic circles (for example, Hadrumetum, now Sousse, in Tunisia, and Lérins, an island monastery off the shore modern-day Cannes, France) where monks wondered how to reconcile their commitment to asceticism with the danger of quietism entailed in Augustine's conviction that "human effort in the here and now had no discernible bearing on a person's eschatological destiny."[61] In his Conference 13, Cassian is keen to maintain that "both grace and human will must be 'free' and cooperating,

---

[60] See Irena Backus and Aza Goudriaan, "'Semipelagianism': The Origins of the Term and its Passage into the History of Heresy," *Journal of Ecclesiastical History* 65 (2014): 25-46.

[61] Conrad Leyser, "Semi-Pelagianism" in Allan D. Fitzgerald, ed., *Augustine through the Centuries: An Encyclopedia* (Grand Rapids: Eerdmans, 1999), 762.

even though the scope of free will is necessarily limited."
[62] He states "that sometimes God requires or looks for (*vel exigat vel expectet*) some effort (*conatus*) of good will before conferring special gifts of grace (*Conf.* 13.13.1). This possibility of the 'initiative of good will' or 'deed' (*initium bonae voluntatis/operis*) is Cassian's emblematic assertion" and reflects "the optimistic anthropology of [his] eastern formation."[63]

Prosper of Aquitaine pounced on the unsuspecting Cassian with a flurry of pamphlets and took upon himself the task of alerting Augustine about a possible resurgence of Pelagianism in the south of France. Augustine immediately replied with two treatises (*De Predestinatione sanctorum* and *De dono perseverantiae*) which are interesting for our purpose here only for one reason: even though the risk of a resurgence of Pelagianism was a fabrication and whatever one makes of Cassian's clumsy assertions on free will, it is undeniable that Augustine's main concern was justified, namely the need to single out and neutralize spiritual elitism. This is why Augustine displayed such relentless commitment

> to the view that no person, group, or institution could assert a reliable insight into the workings of God's grace in human affairs after the incarnation. At the Second Coming the shape and number of the citizens of heaven would be revealed, but in the meantime, moral self-advertisement of

---

[62] Columba Stewart, *Cassian the Monk* (New York/Oxford: Oxford University Press, 1998), 80.

[63] Stewart, *Cassian the Monk*, 80.

> any form — from Donatis, Pelagians, or orthodox ascetics — Augustine decried as theologically ill-founded and socially divisive… Augustine's teaching on predestination, the psychological implications of which continue to baffle and dismay his modern readers, had a specific pastoral goal in the early fifth century: to disabuse unwarranted claims to privileged moral status on the part of communities and their leaders.
>
> Cassian both shared in Augustine's concern about the moral dangers of elitism and sought quite a different solution… His response, however, was not to distrust the ascetic project itself, but to make all the more exacting and precise the means of assessing a person's integrity.[64]

This point is crucial for our topic because the main argument of this paper is that Benedict shares Augustine's concern about the dangers of moral elitism. This explains his increasing wariness towards what we have called the "individual and ascensional" ascetic model inherited from Cassian and Evagrius and is the reason he insulates monastic spirituality against the temptations exemplified by the idea that some monastics might come to see themselves as "self-reliant now" and capable "without the support of another, they are ready. . . to grapple single-handed with the vices of body and mind."[65] He must have reached this conclusion independently from Augustine, as a result of his own experience, but subsequently this might be part of the explanation of why the Augustinian wave powerfully resonated with him when it reached him.

---

[64] Leyser, "Semi-Pelagianism," 763-764.

[65] RB 1.5; Fry, ed., *RB 1980*, 169.

Perfection vs. Holiness

Augustine's aversion to moral and spiritual elitism in his ascetical teaching also permeates his theology of the church and this connection offers interesting avenues to explore the relevance of the aspects of early monasticism we have highlighted so far for the life of our parish communities today.

In many ways the social, political, and spiritual reasons that led to the birth of monasticism in the East are also the triggers of the Pelagian controversy in the West. The main pastoral challenge Augustine faced during his ministry as a bishop resulted from the edict of the emperor Theodosius (380) which proclaimed Christianity as the only religion of the empire. This inevitably led to mass opportunistic conversions to Christianity, and generated a new problem for Christianity, namely a strained cohabitation between sincere practitioners of faith and nominal Christians. Augustine has to warn catechumens that they will see more and more scandals in the Church:

> For you are not unaware that many who have the name of Christians do commit all these evil things that I have briefly mentioned. Neither are you unaware that men whom you know to be called Christians sometimes commit perhaps even graver offenses. . . For He foretold these things, and says in the Gospel: Not every one [*sic*] that saith to me, Lord, Lord, shall enter into the kingdom of heaven, but he that doth [*sic*] the will of my Father. Many will say to me in that day, Lord, Lord, in thy name we have eaten and drunk.[66]

---

[66] Augustine of Hippo, *De catechizandis rudibus* 25, 48; Joseph P. Christopher, trans., *St. Augustine : The First Catechetical Instruction* (New York:

While warning against the dangers of these behaviors however, Augustine does not recommend any attempt to expel these people and is wary of anything that smacks of judgment or moral superiority of one group of Christians over the others. On the contrary, the leitmotiv of his teaching in this regard echoes the sentence we have seen in RB 72.5: "supporting with the greatest patience one another's weaknesses of body or behavior."[67] Tirelessly, Augustine promotes patience as the ecclesial virtue and the most effective spiritual remedy for these challenges:

> For *on this account is God long-suffering towards these,* both that He may strengthen the faith and wisdom of His own elect by trying it through their forwardness, and because many of their number advance and taking pity on their own souls turn with great earnestness to the pleasing of God.[68]

It is in the response to this crisis that Pelagius (d. 418) mostly differs from Augustine.

Pelagius is anxious to restore a strong meaning to the name "Christian" and this is why he prefers to speak of the "perfect Christian." This also explains why he downplays the efficacy of baptism: only those who show their faith with their behavior truly belong to the Church. Baptism is a strictly symbolic gesture and should be administered in response to the merits of the individual. The words that accompany this

Newman Press, 1978), 80.

[67] Fry, ed., *RB 1980,* 295

[68] Augustine of Hippo, *De catechizandis rudibus* 25, 48; Christopher, trans., *St. Augustine : The First Catechetical Instruction,* 80.

sacrament are seen primarily as an exhortation. In theory, Pelagianism proclaims the same requirement of perfection for all. In fact, it ends up in elitism: its own logic leads it from the idea that all Christians must be perfect to the idea that only the perfect are Christians. The fact that this might apply – and indeed appeal – only to a minority strengthens its claims because it favors the "little remnant" mentality, a pride capable of nourishing perseverance. One of the most useful rewards for a minority is the conviction of forming an elite.[69] Hence the Pelagians' taste for visibility and their tendency to judge those whom they see as weak.[70] While Pelagius warns Celantia that she may become more and more lonely as she advances on the road to perfection,[71] Augustine thinks that as we grow in authentic holiness we detect holiness more widely around us.[72]

Thus, while Pelagius seems to be interested only in the maximum that attracts the elites, Augustine emphasizes the minimum required from and accessible to all. In his teaching, Augustine constantly displays a certain benevolence towards the weakest and the concern not to discourage anyone. In the end, while Pelagius favors a moral criterion to determine who truly belongs to the church, Augustine opts for more objective criteria, namely baptism and the confession of faith, and leaves to God the judgment

---

[69] Cf. Jean-Marie Salamito, *Les virtuoses et la multitude : aspects sociaux de la controverse entre Augustin et les pélagiens* (Grenoble : Millon, 2005).

[70] Augustine of Hippo, Ep. 157.5.37.

[71] Pelagius, *Ad Celant.* 2.2.

[72] Augustine of Hippo, *Exposition on Psalm* 34.2.10.

as to who is a real Christian and who is not. This is why, as we have seen already, even in relation to his doctrine of predestination, Augustine's insistence on the secrecy and invisibility of divine election precludes the possibility of constituting a socially identifiable elite of virtuous people who can claim to be predestined.[73]

In the confrontation between Pelagius and Augustine, therefore, we find a wider ecclesial version of the tension between what we have called an "individual and ascensional" model versus the "participatory" model epitomized by the *omnes partier*; that is, reaching the finishing line "all together," as favored by the RB. Among the factors that led both Augustine and Benedict to opt for the latter model, there was a greater wisdom and realism resulting from self-knowledge and pastoral experience.

Before drawing some conclusions from this overview we have one last fascinating observation to make; namely, that it is possible to detect the transition from the "ascensional" to the "participatory" models in Augustine's writings in ways very similar to those we have seen at work in RB.

We saw earlier that, on the wake of his reading of the *Life of Antony*, when Augustine converted to Christianity, he chose to embrace a form of ascetical life, which took the form of common life but was also tinged with a marked yearning for perfection. From this latter viewpoint, at that stage his ideal was not dissimilar to the model that Benedict

---

[73] Augustine of Hippo, *On Admonition and Grace* 16.49.

associates to eremitic life and inherits from Cassian. This appears especially in Augustine's *On the Lord's Sermon on the Mount*, which he wrote very early after his baptism, in 391, and in which he presents a synthesis of the ascent of the soul to God (there we have the "ascensional" tendency again) based on the eight beatitudes of Matthew's gospel, the Lord's prayer, and the gifts of the Holy Spirit: in short, something similar to the seventh chapter of RB on humility. Now, at that stage of his thought, Augustine believed that it was possible to attain a form of ascetical perfection in this life which he describes in ways that strongly resembles Evagrius' *apatheia*, "passionlessness": "Wisdom coincides with the peacemakers, for with peacemakers all things are in proper order, and no passion is in rebellion against reason, but everything is in submission to man's spirit because that spirit is obedient to God. Here it is said of them: *'Blessed are the peacemakers.'*"[74]

Very soon, however, as he went deeper in his reading of Scripture, and as a result of the thinking required especially by the anti-Pelagian polemic, Augustine came to realize that Romans 7:23 ("another law in my members fighting against the law of my mind, captivating me in the law of sin which is in my members") refers to humans not only before their conversion, but even after they have become Christians, and until their death: "After all, it is not granted

---

[74] Augustine of Hippo, *Commentary on the Lord's Sermon on the Mount* 1.4.11; Denis J. Kavanagh, trans., *Saint Augustine: Commentary on the Lord's Sermon on the Mount* (Washington, DC: Catholic University of America Press, 1951), 28.

even to adults in baptism, unless perhaps by an ineffable miracle of the omnipotent creator, that the law of sin, which is present in the members, struggling against the law of the mind, is completely destroyed and no longer exists."[75] And,

> Concupiscence of the flesh has, after all, a certain activity, even when one does not offer it the assent of the heart so that it might reign there or offer one's members as weapons to carry out its commands. . . .We ought, nonetheless, to want those desires not to exist, even if we cannot attain that goal in the body of this death. For this reason the same apostle also instructs us in another passage, speaking as if he were bringing his own person onto the stage. He says, *For I do not do what I want, but I do what I hate* (Rom 7:19), that is, I have those desires. . . . But since he did not want to have desires and yet had those desires and since he was not enslaved to the same concupiscence by consenting to it, he went on to add, *It is no longer I who do it, but the sin that dwells in me* (Rom 7:20).[76]

In other words, it is not just a question of whether or not we rely on God's grace to achieve a certain degree of blamelessness in our behavior, but that, to use RB's words, the currency we need most is patience with ourselves and with others to deal with the weaknesses of our body and our behavior which we will never overcome in our earthly existence.

---

[75] Augustine of Hippo, *On Punishment and Forgiveness of Sins* 1.39.70;

[76] Augustine of Hippo, *On Marriage and Concupiscence* 1.27.30; Roland J. Teske, trans., *Answer to the Pelagians, II: Marriage and Desire, Answer to the Two Letters of the Pelagians, Answer to Julian* (Hyde Park, NY: New City Press, 1998), 47. Later, at the time when he wrote his *Retractationes*, Augustine reiterated this point. See *Retractationes* 2.37 and *Retractationes* 1.19.1-2.

Thus, the model that emerges from RB implies that there is a difference between perfection and holiness. Perfection entails a focus on individual improvement, on overcoming sinful behaviors, and developing good habits to such an extent that our heart is purified and we are given access to contemplation, that is, some form of direct (or mystical) knowledge of God. Personal union with God is the real aim, and communal love tends to be seen as one of the means that enables the monastic to "ascend" in his spiritual life and reach this end.

Holiness, on the contrary, while aiming at reaching a level of spontaneity and freedom in doing what is good and in loving, is happier to allow for human frailty, whether one's own or of others, not instrumentally or provisionally but structurally and sustainably during our life-time. Communal love, especially under the form of patience with oneself and with others, is not a means to an end, but an end in itself, because love is God.

There is an evident tension between perfection and holiness and the whole of Christian spirituality constantly oscillates between these two poles. Trends of spirituality have leaned towards either of these two poles in turn, while never excluding the other altogether. The genius of the RB lies in the fact that it does not try to resolve this tension theoretically, but practically. It caters for the human longing for self-improvement (or perfection) but gradually, delicately, discreetly; it educates the monastic to find joy in solidarity, moderation, and patience that is ultimately in loving.

"Is Christ divided?" (1 Cor. 1:13): Discerning and Ordering the Ascetic Impulse in Early Christianity

REV. DR. ALEXIS TORRANCE[1]

These conferences are designed not to be only dryly academic, but applicable somehow to daily Christian life. As a scholar of theology but also an Orthodox priest, this is of course music to my ears. Whether I succeed in combining these two as well as I should is another matter, but theology that is not only learned but lived is a crucially important concept. It is also one that thoroughly animates the early monastic movement and the early Church as a whole. Christians of every generation are tasked with acquiring the living water of the Holy Spirit in their lives, and I will be arguing that the monastic ideal as it is formulated and understood in the Christian East testifies to this thirst and this need for living water in an especially powerful (but not exclusive) way. In this first part, I would like to discuss the rise of monasticism in the Christian

---

[1] I would like to thank the Reverend Dr. Greg Peters for so kindly inviting me to contribute to the 2021 Parish Asceticism conference and Nashotah House in general for so generously hosting me.

East as something germane rather than alien to the logic of the Gospel. I will be dealing with both the history of the movement (in broad strokes) but also, and perhaps more importantly, with the theological impetus that characterizes early monasticism. The pitfalls and dangers associated with monasticism by its later detractors, especially among the Reformers, were not unknown to early Christians, and so I will attempt to show how some of these major pitfalls and dangers were discussed or dealt with early on. Once we piece together a picture of early Christian monasticism and its rationale, we will have laid the stage for the second part, which will look more particularly at the potential relevance of monasticism for parish life.

Where, then, does monasticism find its source? The textbook answer is in the person of Anthony the Great (ca. 251-356), who does indeed serve as a founding figure for the institution of monasticism as it was to develop, first in Egypt, then in Palestine and from there throughout the Roman empire and beyond. But while the significance of Anthony and other early monastic pioneers such as Pachomius (d. 348) and the Desert Fathers should not be underestimated; there can be a temptation to sever these figures too sharply from what had come before. Usually, the tendency to emphasize monasticism as an "invention" of the third or fourth centuries goes hand-in-hand with a desire to dismiss it entirely as a kind of aberration of the Christian gospel, an unfortunate innovation that contributed to the decline rather than the propagation of true Christianity.

Thus, in one of his invectives against the practice, John Calvin (d. 1564) could write in the sixteenth century: "Still there was nothing with the Fathers less intended than to establish that kind of perfection which was afterwards fabricated by cowled monks, in order to rear up a species of double Christianity."[2] And again, the inimitable Edward Gibbon, no friend of Christianity himself, sums up this popular attitude with aplomb in the eighteenth century: "This voluntary martyrdom must have gradually destroyed the sensibility both of the mind and body; nor can it be presumed that the fanatics who torment themselves are susceptible of any lively affection for the rest of mankind. A cruel, unfeeling temper has distinguished the monks of every age and country: their stern indifference, which is seldom mollified by personal friendship, is inflamed by religious hatred."[3]

We can detect in these barbed criticisms of monasticism two legitimate concerns with the movement: the first is that it inculcates a two-tiered system among Christians, a kind of elite group (the monks) and another group (the non-monks) who come across as second-class citizens. The second concern is that the extreme forms of renunciation and asceticism espoused by some monks would harden them to the point of becoming psychologically damaged

---

[2] John Calvin, *Institutes of the Christian Religion* 4.13.14; Henry Beveridge, trans., *Institutes of the Christian Religion by John Calvin, Volume Third* (Edinburgh: Calvin Translation Society, 1846), 289.

[3] Edward Gibbon, *Decline and Fall of the Roman Empire, Volume I* (Chicago: Encyclopedia Britannica, 1952), 599.

and unfeeling, full of hatred rather than love. We will have to keep these concerns in mind and see what kind of answers the early material offers in response.

But first, I would like to pause over this larger question of whether monasticism does indeed represent a radical break with earlier Christianity. As I said, in its precise forms and its eventual institutional organization, there is certainly a measure of novelty. Yet, in its inner logic, I would argue it is anything but novel or new. The ascetic impulse in Christianity was not invented by Anthony. In fact, Anthony's direct inspiration for adopting a monastic form of life, according to his biographer, Athanasius of Alexandria (d. 373) , was Christ's directive which he heard while attending Church: "If thou wilt be perfect, go and sell that thou hast, and give to the poor, and thou shalt have treasure in heaven: and come and follow me" (Matt 19:21).[4] The ascetic impulse displayed by the early monks is, in other words, a corollary of attempting to enact the commandments of Christ. To propose the cleaving of early monasticism from early Christianity risks dividing Christ from his own commandments. This is an ongoing temptation, I think, that all contemporary Christians must confront, and it orbits around the question of what to do with the totalizing demands of the Gospel. How do we explain Christ's summons to absolute self-denial (to the point, as he says, of hating your own life in Luke 14:26), to repentance, to mourning, to watchfulness, to continual

---

[4] See Athanasius of Alexandria, *Life of Anthony*, 2.

prayer, to love for enemies, and to divine perfection without just explaining them away or ignoring them completely? The Gospel is not a feel-good recipe; it is not interchangeable with positivity training or an ethic of self-satisfaction. It is the revelation or apocalypse of God in the world, the in-breaking of the divinity within the confines of history, and simultaneously it is the revelation of the measure of the human being. The Son of God becomes the Son of Man, depicting in our own nature the perfection of divine life and calling all to inherit that same life in and through Himself. This is the basic content of the Christian Gospel. It is nothing cheap or low. Its awesome grandeur surpasses the comprehension of our frail minds and hearts. Jesus Christ stands before us, God in the flesh. He speaks directly to us, giving us commandments of salvation, and with these commandments giving his own strength, by the Holy Spirit, to accomplish them. For without him, we can do nothing. And so monasticism, in its essence, is nothing but one potent reaction of the human being to the message of the Gospel, itself lived out by the power of God, not the powers of human grit or determination. And of course monasticism is not the only reaction, nor even the most prevalent, to the hearing of the Gospel. But this does not make it foreign to the Gospel. If anything, I see in monastic life a precious gift of the Holy Spirit in the Church, a manifestation in time of the life of the age to come, "where they are neither married nor given in marriage, but are as the angels" (Matt. 22:30). The monastics are, at best, a sign of contradiction, a living image of the self-emptying way of Christ that can serve as a lighthouse and orientation for other Christians. But we will have more opportunity to discuss these ideas below.

For now, my point is this: if we take Christ's commandments seriously, then monasticism should not necessarily seem strange. But if we hum and haw about Christ's commandments, and soften them this way or that, reducing their urgency or ignoring many of them in favor of a generic and fluffy ethic of love and kindness, then perhaps monasticism will never make any sense. But the problem in such a case may not be with monasticism itself but with our impoverished understanding of the meaning and purpose of the Christian life.

When we begin to consider the rise of monasticism from the perspective of Christ's commandments, it becomes easier to see how and why the early monks thought of themselves as merely trying to live out the call of the Gospel in their own particular circumstances. Monastic prototypes were not difficult to find, from the desert-dwellers Prophet Elijah and John the Baptist to the choir of Apostles who "had all things in common" and worshipped together daily (Acts 2:44-47). Paul was an especially good prototype, since he upheld the unmarried state as an ideal (1 Cor. 7:7), brought his body into subjection (1 Cor. 9:27), prayed without ceasing (1 Thess. 5:17), and spent several secret years of withdrawal after his initial conversion (cf. Gal 1:17, Acts 9-11). The ultimate monastic prototype, however, was Christ himself, who must be the source and destination of all Christian striving. Jesus Christ, whose embodiment of perfect chastity, poverty, and obedience, traced out the contours of the monastic vows and gave them their meaning. Without Christ, monasticism would be meaningless vanity. Together with Christ as the fountainhead of the monastic impulse, later Eastern ascetic literature would also dwell on the Virgin Mary as an exemplar of this form of life. For if the goal was union with Christ, who better to uphold as a role model than the one who bore the very Word of God in the flesh? She did so, moreover, in virginity, in poverty, in obedience.

The rise of monasticism, once again, does not arise from nowhere, nor straightforwardly from some extraneous pagan culture. Apart from some very few exceptions (including Second Temple apocalyptic Jewish groups such as the Essenes), this way of life was virtually unknown in the ancient world. It is also not exclusively to be associated with the toleration and eventual adoption of Christianity by the Roman empire, though this did provide suitable conditions for its codification and expansion. The path of virginity in the service of Christ was seen as part and parcel of the witness of the early Church. By *witness* (*martyria* in Greek) we should understand the full meaning of that term, which includes the connotation of *martyrdom*. In fact, in his defense of the Christian faith over against the pagan world, Athanasius of Alexandria makes the case that a kind of proof of the truth and glory of Christ's Gospel can be seen in the combination of literal martyrs who die for Christ and "in the virgins of Christ, and in the young men who practice chastity as part of their religion."[5] In both cases, their faith in Christ proves to be stronger than death, stronger than the pull of this world, and so a kind of continuation of Christ's work, of putting death to death and transfiguring the world. The theme of monks as a kind of martyr, "dying daily" for the Gospel (cf. 1 Cor. 15:31), became commonplace but not because real martyrdoms completely ceased and needed to be replaced by something else. Throughout Church history there have existed both these forms of witness, of "martyrdom." They are, however, but the most dramatic and historically revered forms of one and the same quest common to every Christian, which is to be wholly conformed to Our Lord.

We would do well to consider not only how monks have been described from the outside, but how monks have understood themselves and their own calling.[6] The word "monk" is an interesting place to start. It comes from the Greek word *monachos*, which literally means a "solitary," someone who is alone. This appears to be a counter-intuitive description for a Christian way of life. Are not Christians called to a life not of solitude, but radical communion? Indeed, communion and relationality are

[5] Athanasius of Alexandria, *On the Incarnation* 48; A Religious of C. S. M. V., trans., *On the Incarnation: The Treatise De incarnatione Verbi Dei* (Crestwood, NY: St. Vladimir's Seminary Press, 1944), 85.

[6] For more on this question, see Alexis Torrance, "Individuality and Identity-Formation in Late Antique Monasticism" in Alexis Torrance and Johannes Zachhuber, eds., *Individuality in Late Antiquity* (Aldershot, UK: Ashgate, 2014), 111-127.

constitutive of the Christian message of what it means not only to be human, but also what it means to be divine. However, *what kind* of communion and relationship are we talking about? Yes, Jesus Christ ministered in cities, towns, and villages, but he also repeatedly went out into the desert alone, even at one point for forty days and forty nights. John the Baptist, declared by Christ to be the greatest prophet born of women (Luke 7:28; cf. Matt. 11:11), led his ministry exclusively, from what we can gather, out of the desert. Are these exceptions to the rule of communion and relationship, or might they tell us something deeper about the true nature of communion and relationship? Eastern monastic writers have wrestled with this dilemma since the beginning. A popular saying attributed to the early desert father Alonas ran like this: "if the human being does not say in his heart, 'God and I are alone in this world,' he will not find peace."[7] The acquisition of peace, a word which in Greek (*irene*) also means wholeness or completeness, was associated first and foremost with a total focus on the relationship of the monk's heart with his Creator. This was considered an anchor that held the monk close to the source of true communion and relationality while setting aside any and all counterfeits and crutches of the world that could not bring real peace to the heart, real wholeness. But such an approach could never be permitted to slip into narcissism or self-absorption. Evagrius of Pontus defines the *monachos*,

---

[7] *Apophthegmata Patrum* (alphabetical collection), Alonas 1 (PG 64.133A); my translation. See also found Barsanuphius and John of Gaza, *Letter* 346 (SC 450:360). Unless otherwise noted, all translations are my own.

the solitary one, as someone who, "though separated from all, is united to all."[8] Clearly, he recognized the potential problem and criticism associated with the term "monk" and tried to show its Christian meaning. He considers blessed the monk "who regards every human being as a god after God" and "who looks on the salvation and progress of all as though they were his own, with joy."[9] That is, the escape from the world implied within monastic life, was not an escape from community or the other, least of all from love. It was considered a means of finding a better and truer communion, a relationship with God and neighbor built, as Dionysius the Areopagite (ca. 5th-6th c.) describes it, on "the science of the unifying commandments."[10]

Nonetheless, we do see a tension here, a paradox, which is not an unusual thing in Christian theology. The monk is still called to radical solitude even while upholding the ideals of communion and relationship. So on the one hand, the monk is, in the words of Maximus the Confessor (d. 662) and John Climacus (d. 649), "he who has withdrawn his mind from sensory objects and who ceaselessly cleaves to God by self-mastery, love, psalmody and prayer"[11]; "who strictly controls his nature and unceasingly watches over his

---

[8] Evagrius of Pontus, *De Oratione* 124 (PG 79.1193C): μοναχός ἐστιν, ὁ πάντων χωρισθείς, καὶ πᾶσι συνηρμοσμένος.

[9] Evagrius of Pontus, *De Oratione* 122-123 (PG 79.1193BC).

[10] Dionysius the Areopagite, *Ecclesiastical Hierarchy* 6.3.2 (PG 3.533D): ἐν ἐπιστήμη τῶν ἑνοποιῶν ἐντολῶν ἐνεργουμένην.

[11] Maximus the Confessor, *Chapters on Love* 2.54 (PG 90.1001C).

senses,"[12] and who is "a willing exile from his home."[13] Yet on the other hand, he is "united to all" in this very act of exile; though in some sense distant from all, he is devoting his life to the commandment to love all.[14] This paradox might be described as "the solidarity of the solitary." It is described beautifully already by Serapion of Thmuis (d. 362), a disciple of Anthony the Great, who on the latter's death celebrates the potency of Anthony's monastic life not simply for Anthony's own relationship and communion with God, but because it begat in him prayer "for the whole world," a prayer that truly uplifted, protected, and sustained the world in a way few could understand.[15]

This tension between being "not of the world" yet "for the world and its salvation," is the subject of a poetic meditation in an anonymous early Syriac Christian homily entitled *On hermits and desert dwellers*. There we read about the uncompromising isolation of such people in the desert, who commune there with the spiritual world: "They see only animals instead of people; and instead of families they left behind, angels come down to them." But the text goes

---

[12] John Climacus, *Ladder of Divine Ascent* 1.4 (PG 88.633C); *Saint John Climacus: The Ladder of Divine Ascent, Revised Edition* (Boston: Holy Transfiguration Monastery, 1991), 4, slightly modified.

[13] John Climacus, *Ladder of Divine Ascent* 3.8 (PG 88.665A); *Saint John Climacus: The Ladder of Divine Ascent*, 15.

[14] Cf. Isaac the Syrian, *Homily* 64; D. Miller (trans.), Dana Miller, trans., *The Ascetical Homilies of St. Isaac the Syrian* (Brookline MA: Holy Transfiguration Monastery, 1984), 307-308.

[15] See René Draguet, "Une lettre de Sérapion de Thmuis aux disciples d'Antoine (A.D. 356) en versions syriaque et arménienne," *Le Muséon* 64 (1951): 1225.

on to emphasize their communion and relationship not simply vertically with God and the heavenly realm, but also horizontally, with the world at large:

> When their tears stream down, they banish harm from the earth; and when their petition is raised, it fills the world with assistance. . . . The wilderness that everyone fears has become a great place of refuge for them, where assistance flows from their bones to all creation. . . . Civilization, where lawlessness prevails, is sustained by their prayers. And the world, buried in sin, is preserved by their prayers.[16]

Such sentiments regarding the inestimable benefit *for* the world of this form of prayerful withdrawal *from* the world are echoed throughout the Eastern monastic tradition down to our own day. The twentieth-century monk and saint of the Orthodox Church, Silouan of Mount Athos (d. 1938), even sees this work of monasticism as *constitutive* of what it means to be a monk: "A monk is someone who prays for the whole world, who weeps for the whole world; and in this lies his main work."[17] He goes on to elaborate:

> But who is it constrains him to weep for the whole world? The Lord Jesus Christ, Son of God, incites him. He gives the monk the love of the Holy Spirit, and by virtue of this love the monk's heart forever sorrows over the people because not all men are saved. The Lord Himself so grieved over people that He gave Himself to death on the Cross.[18]

---

[16] [Ephraim], *On hermits and desert dwellers* 105, 497 and 501; Joseph P. Amar in Vincent Wimbush, ed., *Ascetic Behavior in Greco-Roman Antiquity: A Sourcebook* (Minneapolis: Fortress Press, 1990), 70 and 79.

[17] Saint Sophrony, *Saint Silouan the Athonite*, trans. Rosemary Edmonds (Crestwood, NY: St. Vladimir's Seminary Press, 2021), 407.

[18] Sophrony, *Saint Silouan the Athonite*, 407.

Notice the importance in Silouan's rationale for the monastic life accorded to the governing roles of Christ and the Holy Spirit. Monasticism is a divine gift from on high. Outwardly, it is manifest in the abandonment of all things of this world for the sake of Jesus Christ ("Go and sell that thou hast, and give to the poor, and come and follow me" – Matt. 19:21). Yet, as we see here, its positive meaning is found in intercessory prayer, bearing the burdens of the world by holding them up continually in supplication to God, through the love of the Holy Spirit, thereby following Our Lord Jesus Christ himself, who laid his life for all. This is the monk's highest nourishment: not some form of psychological peace or tranquility that one might find on the yoga mat, but the active and burning strain of the soul to conform to Christ-likeness, which inevitably means the path of the Life-giving Cross on behalf of all and for all.[19]

So, although withdrawn from society, monks have never understood themselves to be withdrawing out of hatred or contempt for other people: it is the love of God that serves as the driving force in their self-understanding. Of course, I have focused on the more extreme form of monasticism so far, the solitary or eremitical life. Most monks down the ages, have not belonged to this harsher category. In tandem with the life of Anthony the Great, in fact, we see the rise in Church history of a more communal form of monasticism, associated with the name of Pachomius the

---

[19] I examine this idea in some detail in Alexis Torrance, *Repentance in Late Antiquity: Eastern Asceticism and the Framing of the Christian Life, ca. 400–650* (Oxford: Oxford University Press, 2013), esp. chs. 4–6.

Great. Pachomius was instrumental in forging monastic communities of monks and nuns, sharing all things in common after the model of the Apostles in Acts 2, with Church worship forming the heart of this communal life, around which everything else in the monastery orbited. Rules for these monasteries were drawn up, which regulated the governing structure of the monastery, the different roles played by different office-holders, the frequency of meals, the hours of prayer, rest, and so on. Of course, these early Christian monastic rules ultimately lie behind the famous rule of Benedict in the West. In the East, no one rule ever really gained the same prominence as the RB, although they tended to share many commonalities. Instead, each monastery would (usually through the initiative of a founding abbot) institute a rule or *typicon* that drew on earlier models but was adapted to the specific monastery in question. The most famous early Christian rule (which in turn directly influenced Benedict's) was that of Basil the Great (d. 379) in the fourth century, a towering figure of the early Church. To this day, his guidelines and counsels have made their mark on virtually every Eastern Christian monastic rule.

Together with the solitary and fully communal forms of monastic life, we also find in the early period something in between and hybrid models. Thus, the way of life of the majority of those figures we refer to as the Desert Fathers was not quite fully communal, but nor was it solitary in the fullest sense of that term. Instead, an elderly monk might have one or two disciples living in a simple dwelling, with several other such dwellings and arrangements in the vicinity. This was known as a skete, where during the week each dwelling was relatively self-sufficient (with one or a handful of monks in each), but at the weekends all the monks would gather at a central Church for the celebration of the Holy Eucharist on Saturdays and Sundays, as well as a common meal. Some, such as John Climacus, tentatively commended this middle path as perhaps the most desirable form of monasticism, combining the best of both worlds, although he also assumes the need for discernment in each individual case.[20]

As monasticism developed in the East, we see hybrid forms developing. Eventually, we begin to find (and still do today), larger coenobitic or communal monasteries that include clusters of sketes or hermitages under its protection. In such an arrangement, it might not be uncommon for a monk to begin in the coenobitic monastery and later to receive a blessing to live a more isolated life in a cell with one or two others, or even alone, yet always with that special connection (for both spiritual and material needs) to the main monastery. There is an acknowledgment, in other words, that monasticism should not be construed as a one-size-fits-all endeavor. As a form of life, it is circumscribed, of course, by the vows of obedience, poverty, and chastity, but each monastic community, skete, and hermitage fulfils this way of life in its own distinct manner.

---

[20] John Climacus, *Ladder of Divine Ascent*, Step 1.26.

I mentioned the pioneering efforts of Anthony and Pachomius, as well as the influence of Basil's rule on Eastern monasticism. But other crucial figures also helped give shape and content to Eastern monasticism. Euthymius the Great helped set monasticism in the area of Palestine on a firm footing in the early fifth century, followed by Sabas the Sanctified (d. 532). The latter's monastery, known as Mar Sabas, is one of the oldest continuously active monasteries in the world, founded in 483. Another contender is the Monastery of St Catherine at Mount Sinai. In both cases, these monasteries have been instrumental in passing on the monastic way of life to subsequent generations far and wide, as well as being hubs for the development of liturgy, the production of hymnography (the theologian and hymnographer John of Damascus [d. ca. 749], for instance, was a monk of Mar Saba), and repositories for ancient scriptural and patristic manuscripts. The most influential detailed approach to coenobitic or communal monasticism in the East came from Theodore the Studite in the early ninth century, whose rule or typicon (itself influenced by Basil, Mar Saba, and others), became a basis for the famous monasteries on Mount Athos. Mount Athos, a semi-autonomous monastic republic, is a peninsula in Northern Greece that still houses some twenty communal monasteries and many sketes and hermitages. There the daily celebration of the Divine Liturgy (the Holy Eucharist) is a hallmark of the monks' way of life.

The mention of the worship of the Church brings

us to another critical point when it comes to the history and nature of monasticism. That is its relationship to the institutional Church. As alluded to earlier, this has always been a bone of contention, especially among the detractors of monasticism, who perceive it as raising a double standard of elite and true Christianity over against a soft and perhaps even false Christianity: a form, in other words, of works righteousness. This is not a new problem, nor one discovered by the sixteenth-century Protestant Reformers. Several movements in early Christianity erred in this direction. The most relevant one for our purposes is known as Messalianism, from the Syriac word for prayer: Messalians were "those who pray." The problem, of course, was not that they prayed. The problem was that they put their confidence in their own prayer as the source of sanctification and salvation. They formed ascetic communities that tended to denigrate and despise ordinary Christians as not quite the full shilling. Not only that, but their confidence in their own prayer and ascetic feats was such that they looked down on the institutional Church as a whole as well as her sacraments. They argued, for instance, that baptism was at best a shaving off the surface evils attached to someone, but that it did not really root out evil from the heart nor transform the person in any deep or meaningful way. Deep and meaningful change could only, for the Messalians, come from one's own efforts to drive out one's inner demon, and it depended on an ascetic life of celibacy and unceasing prayer.

The Messalian temptation has taken many different forms and continues to be an issue in some circles. But it is not the face of monasticism itself, and certainly not the monasticism that was ratified and celebrated by the institutional Church. A key early theologian who helped unveil and defeat the Messalian temptation was Mark the Monk, or Mark the Ascetic, writing probably in the first half of the sixth century.[21] One of St. Mark's principal tactics was to root all of Christian life not in human effort but in the work and Church of Christ, and especially the sacraments of the Church that freely renew and heal human beings. He even wrote a treatise against those who claim to be justified by works! Some early Lutherans took an interest in this text, incidentally, but it was quietly dropped when they realized how much emphasis Mark still put on the active keeping of Christ's commandments. His point against the Messalians was not to say that the monastic life or keeping the commandments in general were themselves useless but that the positive source, ground, and basis for all Christian striving *is not ourselves but the work of God in Christ*, a work ongoing in the Church. The nature of baptism, in particular, provided the most potent argument for St. Mark against the elitist tendencies of the Messalians. Mark saw in baptism a new and free birth from above, the death of the old self and the putting on of Christ. Baptism did not simply constitute a first and optional baby step from which that monastic life

---

[21] For more on St. Mark and his theology, see Torrance, *Repentance in Late Antiquity*, 88-117.

went on to take over. Baptism contained the fullness of the mystery of salvation, the fullness of perfection. No amount of ascetic striving could justify, earn, or approximate this gratuitous and unmerited gift. This position guaranteed an equivalency among *all* Christians that no amount of monastic virtuosity could match. Yet, one might ask, if baptism really does impart the perfection of the gift of Christ, why have monasticism at all or, indeed, any of the other sacraments?

Mark addresses this quite eloquently by distinguishing between the reception of the fullness of grace in baptism in a hidden or mystical way, and the active manifestation of that fullness through life in the Church and the keeping of the Gospel commandments. As he summarizes his position, "all that have been baptized in an orthodox manner have received the whole of grace mystically, but they afterwards receive full assurance through the keeping of the commandments."[22] Kallistos Ware states succinctly that "around these two terms μυστικῶς [mystically/in a hidden manner] and ἐνεργῶς [actively], the whole of Mark's ascetic and mystical theology is centred."[23] What Mark is doing is ultimately safeguarding both the significance of monasticism but also its theological subservience and dependence on the larger institutional Church. No one can baptize themselves: it is an ecclesial act, and a supremely

---

[22] Mark the Monk, *No Justification by Works* 85 (SC 445:156).

[23] Kallistos Ware, *The Ascetic Writings of Mark the Hermit* (DPhil thesis, University of Oxford, 1965), 229.

corporate act at that, constituting an *incorporation* into Christ's saving Body. Yet, although it represents a real fullness of grace, it is also a beginning—a beginning of the manifestation of that grace through the keeping of Christ's commandments. The keeping of Christ's commandments in Mark's mind is not limited, of course, to monastic life (this would ultimately undermine his argument), and it encompasses the other sacraments (the Eucharist, for instance, which fulfils the command to "do this in remembrance of me"). The commandments are not a legal code but the manifestation of the divine life ("be perfect, as your Father in heaven is perfect" – Matt. 5:48). As Mark puts it, "the Lord is hidden in his own commandments, and he is to be found there in the measure that he is sought."[24] As such, the commandments cannot be truly kept by us through determination or grit, contrary to the Messalians' claim. God must work in us to fulfil them. And in Christian life, his work begins definitively through holy baptism, whose strength equips our will, enlightens our minds, and strengthens our hearts for the service of divine love that characterizes all the commandments. This is why Mark can say that even after baptism, the commandments are only ever fulfilled "by the mercies of Our Lord Jesus Christ."[25]

On a theological level, then, the early monks came quickly to the defense of the Church and its primacy vis-à-vis their way of life. An ascetic Christian life that is not

---

[24] Mark the Monk, *On the Spiritual Law*, 191 (SC 445:124).

[25] Mark the Monk, *On the Spiritual Law*, 30 (SC 445:82).

an *ecclesial* life was understood by Mark and others to be a dangerous fiction, a recipe for self-made religion that used the Christian moniker only as a convenient guise. But there were also legislative safeguards enacted by the Church as the monastic movement spread. Some of these are in evidence at the Fourth Ecumenical Council at Chalcedon in 451, where several of the disciplinary canons there make clear that any monastic community, like the parishes, must consider itself to be under the jurisdiction and supervision of the local bishop. The path of monasticism was understood primarily as a path of repentance (we will discuss this more in the next part), so if anything, the monastic communities were expected to be more deferential to the institutional Church than the simple parishes. Clearly, the tensions lying behind the early disciplinary canons indicate that a harmonious co-existence between bishop and monastery was not always in evidence. And that tension has always been present to varying degrees. Yet the basic message is clear and rather similar to Mark's argument. The monastery is a legitimate manifestation of the Christian life, even a rather powerful one, but its legitimacy and efficacy *depend on its belonging to the local church*. Without this connection to the institution, it loses its claims to legitimacy. Now, there have of course been thorny issues and grey areas in Church history on this matter, especially during times of doctrinal conflict (for instance during the iconoclast controversy). But even then, the cardinal importance of the connection between the monastery and the Church, and that the former does not simply coincide with the latter, was always presupposed.

In other words, together with the ascetic impulse that has always been present in Christianity, there has likewise always been a recognition that asceticism is not a self-sufficient tool. It needs Christ to be successful, and as such, it needs the Church. This ascetic impulse is manifested diversely in Christianity. One can make a compelling case that marriage contains within itself an ascetic calling too. But in this paper we have been dealing primarily with the monastic manifestation of asceticism, its history, and its logic. Jesus Christ is the only legitimate end, the *telos*, of all Christian striving, of all Christian asceticism. He is not divided, as Paul insisted, even if the members of His Body and their paths to Him are wondrously diverse. Neither monasticism nor married life are monoliths. They have their basic form and structure, of course, a form and structure already traced in outline within the New Testament. But each and every human being that embraces the path of monasticism or, for that matter, marriage, is embracing a deeply personal and unrepeatable journey that has as its aim the acquisition of the mind of Christ, the life of Christ, which can be received not by any human effort but by the condescension of the Holy Spirit.

Let me conclude this first part by returning to the theme of the monk as solitary, someone who is alone. As I mentioned, the potential misrepresentation of the purpose of monasticism contained within this term was not lost on the monks themselves. Among the most beautiful expressions of the inadequacy of the term was expressed in a poem by the eleventh-century monk and theologian Symeon the New Theologian (d. 1022).[26] In Hymn 27, he meditates on the monk as someone who is, by definition, "alone." He finds the term *monachos* dissatisfying and misleading. Strictly speaking, he says, the monk is only truly such when "Christ the King" dwells within him. And yet, he argues, "in such a case you are not alone [οὐ μονάζων], for the king lives with you."[27] The monk is only "alone" in a relative sense, namely in the eyes of the world, but "since you are united to the king and God, you are not alone, but are numbered among all the saints."[28] He continues his line of argument, asking, "if then someone has Christ abiding within him, how is it possible, tell me, to call him 'solitary' [μόνος]?"[29] The one who is truly alone, he goes on, is the one who is separated from God. Being separated from God is then linked to a separation from other human beings:

> Each one of us is completely
> separated from other human beings,
> and all of us are isolated like orphans,
> even if we appear to be united by virtue of living together
> and mixing with one another in this numerous assembly.[30]

---

[26] For what follows and its fuller discussion, see Alexis Torrance, *Human Perfection in Byzantine Theology: Attaining the Fullness of Christ* (Oxford: Oxford University Press, 2020), 144-149.

[27] Symeon the New Theologian, Hymn 27.6 (SC 174:278; ed. Kambylis, 236).

[28] Symeon the New Theologian, Hymn 27.10 (SC 174:278; ed. Kambylis, 236).

[29] Symeon the New Theologian, Hymn 27.18–19 (SC 174:280; ed. Kambylis, 236).

[30] Symeon the New Theologian, Hymn 27.28–32 (SC 174:280; ed. Kambylis, 237).

In this profound meditation, Symeon upends our expectations about the term "monk." It is only in relation to the worldly order of things that the monk appears to be such. On closer examination, it is really those in the world, hankering after the fleeting desires and pleasures of this life, who are the monks, the solitaries. Their apparently intense communities and network of relationships are but a mirage for Symeon, a façade that hides the endemic loneliness and isolation that characterizes the human being estranged from God. His proof of this, is the fact that corruption and death inevitably come to swallow up all this superficial communion and these relationships: "death shows that this is true … and it dissolves the unity of the crowds."[31] Symeon asks us to look deeper, to see that our tendency to recoil at the monastic life as an abnormal rejection of relationship and communion may in fact be concealing an insecurity within us. This insecurity is the realization of our own inner isolation, however much we fill our lives with superficial relationships, friendships, parties, and so on. It is we, on this reading, that are the monks. And not in a good way. We are alone. Not because we have fled towards God but away from him. The true monk once again stands as a sign of contradiction, a witness to the fact that in being "alone" in a worldly sense but for the sake of God, he has gained everything, love for God and love for neighbor, which is another way of saying communion with God and

---

[31] Symeon the New Theologian, Hymn 27.34–38 (SC 174:280–82; ed. Kambylis, 237): τὴν ἕνωσιν τὴν τῶν πολλῶν διαλύει.

communion with neighbor. The Apostle expresses this way of life thus: "As sorrowful, yet always rejoicing; as poor, yet making many rich; as having nothing, and yet possessing all things" (2 Cor. 6:10). If we cease judging according to appearances but judge with righteous judgment as Our Lord exhorts us to do (John 7:24), perhaps we will see that, in the end, our assumptions about monasticism were mistaken. And we can use this realization for our edification, to humble ourselves, to see the poverty of our inner state, our tragic isolation from God, and use this sentiment for the building up of our life in Christ. But if we simply cling to our prejudice about what counts as a Christian life and what does not, we will perhaps let something all too precious for our own spiritual growth, our own salvation, pass us by.

The Rule Of St. Benedict
And Parish Life Today:
Taking Affects and Bodies Seriously

Rev. Dr. Luigi Gioia

To apply the findings of my first paper to contemporary parish life we need to reflect on whether there is something analogous to the tension between perfection and holiness (or between "individual/ ascensional" vs. "participatory" models) in our culture and whether the church has anything to offer in this regard.

We belong to a culture which has secularized the quest for perfection which in most ancient cultures was the realm of religion. The "perfection" we tend to strive for in our time is well-being or "wholeness" at as many levels as possible: physical, emotional, psychological, and often spiritual. Interestingly, in ways not entirely dissimilar from forms of what we have called the "ascensional model," we associate this well-being to a notion of individuality which is a synonym of autonomy and self-referentiality. What is more, our contemporary notion of individuality contains unmistakable Pelagian overtones.

It all started with the search for certainty of Modernity (and by "Modernity" I mean here the age of reason that started with seventeenth- and eighteenth-century Enlightenment). We are painfully aware of the limitations of our perception of reality, of the constant possibility of making mistakes or deluding ourselves. Is there any reality so immediate, self-evident, and undoubtable that I can trust it absolutely? We all know the famous solution given to this dilemma by the French philosopher René Descartes (d. 1650): *Cogito ergo sum*, which can be translated as "Even when I doubt of everything else, including myself and the world, I know that there is me doubting, me questioning, and me thinking – my only certainty is my self-awareness." In other words, *Cogito ergo sum* means "me, me, me"! This "me" is the measure of everything and the arbiter of all values. The whole of reality can be established starting from it. Ultimately, I am in charge of my identity: I become what I decide to be through my choices.

This momentous shift of perception has fundamentally simplified our perception of reality: there are only subjects and objects. We humans are subjects, those who act upon everything else, in a position to overview and control, and we shape reality. Everything else, including other human beings sometimes, are "objects," that are "acted upon," things we can delimit, describe, handle, put to use. There is no denying that this approach has given us great power and effectiveness: the whole technological revolution on which our present well-being rests was made possible by this approach to reality.

From this viewpoint, therefore, well-being means being autonomous, self-referential, and in control. There is no other reality than that which can be known empirically and exploited with the help of technology. If there are other aspects of reality, they are optional and ultimately superfluous, they can be left to our free time, like hobbies, when the serious business is over. Among these unnecessary realities, as we know, we have relegated God, interiority, the environment, and other negligible things like wonder, compassion, and grace.

This has an impact on the way in which we perceive ourselves as individuals in relation to other individuals and to the world – that is, on our perception of communities. We are happy to cooperate with others on the basis of facts; that is, of what we can be sure of from the scientific or pragmatic viewpoint, but we leave aside everything else, especially beliefs and values, because they cannot be proved, are too subjective, divisive, and ultimately irrelevant. We only need to agree with others on their rights – and ours: we will not encroach on their individual freedom, and we expect them do the same with us.

This is a very sketchy description, but it should be enough to help us in dealing with the question of what difference does the Christian message make in this context, what is the contribution which our parishes, our Christian communities can give in this context. We can start by acknowledging what we owe to the mindset I have just outlined. When we think about what life standards were throughout much of human history, there is no denying that we are lucky to live in our time. Despite the persistence of huge inequalities, there has never been a better period for life expectancy, health, nourishment, education, free time, travelling, upward mobility, social and political freedom. We tend to think that it is only a matter of time before these enhancements are extended to the whole of humanity. During the past century, for the first time in history, the share of people who have access to them (and, therefore, qualify as "middle class") has risen from one-third of the world population to over half. As always, we may choose to see the glass as half empty, but it would be unfair to deny this progress.

This appreciation changes, however, if we ask ourselves whether greater well-being has made individuals flourish, develop their potential, feel fulfilled – in a word whether well-being has contributed to what I would like to call "wholeness."

One of the metaphors we use to describe the risk entailed by any major existential challenge is that it can lead us to "fall apart." The interest of this metaphor is that it portrays human identity in terms of unity, wholeness, and self-containment. It resonates with the etymology of the word "individual": that which is not divisible. Biologically, an individual starts by a process of aggregation of cells in its mother's womb and ceases to exist when it breaks apart with death. We are alive because some mysterious force which we call "life" or "soul" keeps us together, as a unity, physically. In the same way, we flourish emotionally and psychologically by keeping that which makes us unique, distinctive, irreplaceable, recognizable, valued, and hopefully loved, in a coherent and meaningful ensemble, a whole.

So, the question which Christian spirituality should keep alive regarding our identity as individuals is whether our quest for well-being alone makes our lives more meaningful, gives us a sense of wholeness. Of course, some may see this question as a luxury. For people who live in extreme precariousness, just staying alive, eating, finding shelter, and being safe from physical harm is all-consuming—in the fight for survival there is no time for wholeness.

This is why the salvation God promised and realized in the Old Testament is first of all a rescue: he liberates his people from slavery, protects them against the enemy, gives them bread from heaven, water from the rock, and a land where they can settle and live without fear. This is the content of the Lord's blessing promised to Abraham and renewed to all his descendants. When God announces his intention to intervene decisively in favour of his people, however, his aim is not just to ensure their survival or their well-being but something which might sound unnecessary, namely that which Scripture calls worship, or praise, or thanksgiving. In the book of Exodus, God does not simply say to Moses that he wants to take his people out of Egypt (that is what he wants to save them *from*), but that he wants them to be free to worship him on his mountain (that is what he wants to save them *for*).

This is what, from a theological viewpoint, truly makes us whole or, if we want, holy: the freedom to indulge ourselves in thanksgiving. It is not just a question of politeness, of saying thank you for a gift we receive from God. Thanksgiving is so important in Scripture because it is the symbol of what makes human existence responsive, meaningful, and worth living. An image will help us here. According to psychology, one of the crucial ways through which a child perceives itself as a whole, as a unity, and as an individual, is the embrace of its mother and father. Our longing for meaningful and loving embraces during the rest of our life echoes this foundational experience. This is why in times of distress, when we feel threatened to fall apart, embraces are so comforting, from the right people and in the right context, of course. But even more than physical embrace, what restores wholeness are the metaphorical embraces of words of consolation and encouragement, of quality listening, or even just of silent presence and companionship. What makes us whole in life is feeling recognized, valued, and loved. These are the things that put a smile on our faces, give us energy and motivation, make us glow.

Praise and thanksgiving are not just the verbal expressions of a recognition but something analogous to what happens to a celestial body that is caught in the gravitational pull of a star. It stops roaming aimlessly and starts orbiting around the star, feeds on its light and warmth, and, thanks to the circular motion, acquires a spherical shape—literally becoming well-rounded. We never escape God's gravitational pull, of course. In him we have life, movement, and being, as the Apostle Paul says in the Acts of the Apostles. But our sense of identity changes decisively when it is impacted by the embrace of God's Word, when we acquire the ability to recognize him as active and present in our lives and joyously acknowledge our dependence on him.

Modernity wants us to rely on a search for absolute certainty, whereas, at a much deeper level, our identity depends on assurance and validation. Assurance and validation are the true embrace that makes us whole, the mysterious force that allows us, as we say, to "keep it together" and, echoing the prophet Zechariah's words in Luke's gospel, leads us to give praise to the Lord, the God of Israel, who "enables us to serve him without fear, in holiness (and we could say in wholeness) before him all the days of our life" (Luke 1:74-75). This is why, more than well-being, the ultimate sign that we are truly alive and free as individuals is thanksgiving.

The corollary of our modern view of the individual self as autonomous and self-referential is the way we conceive life as a group, whether in our workplace, in civil society, and often even in our churches, based on the principle (which we consider as self-evident) that all human beings have equal worth and therefore equal rights. Individuals come before the group and commit to it only to the extent that they benefit from it. We have duties and must obey rules, but we accept them only as the reverse side of the real advantage we draw from society, that is the protection of our rights. In classical liberalism, these rights are mainly "negative," insofar as their main purpose is to prevent interference in a person's freedom of action and thought. In more recent, mainly European, egalitarian forms of liberalism, this notion has been expanded to include "positive" rights like equality of opportunities and entitlement to the resources necessary to flourish as an individual, in a word what we call the "welfare state."

There is nothing wrong with this, we might think. Indeed, we should be grateful that we live in a culture committed to these principles. The problem with this model, however, is its reluctance to take into account any unifying social factor other than our rights or our entitlements. This is based on the separation between facts and values that I mentioned earlier and which underpins modernity. "Values" are our belief systems, our notions of what is good, and it is true that we often disagree about them – more than ever in our intensely polarized society. Precisely because values and belief systems are so divisive and subjective, as a society we have come to the conclusion that it is better to base our common life on "facts," things so self-evident that they cannot be disputed, at least in principle. Thus, we decided to consider a "fact" that all human beings are equal and therefore that they should all be granted the same rights and, increasingly, the same benefits.

Nothing more is required for social cohesion since the ambition of this model is not heart-felt solidarity but the preservation of individual freedom and equality of opportunity. We do not need friendship, companionship, reciprocal fondness to live together. In fact, we can remain pretty indifferent to most of our fellows, colleagues, even co-religionaries. To function as a group, the only thing we need is making sure we all agree on following the same procedures. Social cohesion is entrusted to a Weberian bureaucratic and managerial framework which churns increasingly detailed regulations and asserts an ever-growing power to enforce them, thanks to the capillary (and frightening) control afforded by our modern digital surveillance state.

Even the staunchest defenders of this model, however, are starting to have some qualms about its narrative. A recent astute and yet self-critical article in *The Economist* acknowledges that "Enlightenment liberalism is losing ground in the debate about race. A new ideology is emerging."[1] Reflecting on the recent surge of racial unrest in the United States and more generally in the Western hemisphere, this essay recognizes that despite its professed commitment to equality of rights and access to resources, liberalism has neglected ethnic minorities, and toyed with racism, imperialism, and paternalism.

Grudgingly, liberalism is accepting the need for

---

[1] See "In the balance: Enlightenment liberalism is losing ground in the debate about how to deal with racism," *The Economist* Vol. 436, Iss. 9202 (July 11, 2020): 53-54,56.

collective action under the form of "group identity": the victims of racial-, gender-, or disability-related discrimination who cannot make their voice heard as individuals have the right to be empowered as groups and claim recognition of their identity. We are moving from a society of competing individuals to another of competing groups, but the logic is the same: it is about establishing rights and making sure that they are enshrined in social behavior, in political correctness, and, of course, in regulations. It does not really matter whether we all agree on the reasons we should respect and support each other. We have given up on trying. To use a sentence from Augustine of Hippo (d. 430) recently brought to prominence by President Joe Biden, we have lost faith in the possibility of ever finding "common objects of love."[2]

It is at this junction that we see the crisis of Modernity compounded by the dead-end of post-Modernity. In a nutshell, Modernity thinks we all are rational beings who can agree on some basic universal and self-evident principles (and human rights belong to this category) and, if not kindly, at least politely rally around them. Post-Modernity claims that any pretense to establish universal and rational principles is just a trick used by whoever is in power at the time to protect and extend their privilege and authority. All we ever do is invent narratives, or stories,

---

[2] See Augustine of Hippo, *City of God* 19.24; and Joseph R. Biden, Jr., "Inaugural Address" (January 20, 2021), available at https://www.whitehou-se.gov/briefing-room/speeches-remarks/2021/01/20/inaugural-address-by-president-joseph-r-biden-jr/.

and make sure enough people believe they are true. Rights, democracy, religions, family values, genre, group identities are all stories, all tricks, none of them are intrinsically true. A story takes the upper hand only because some categories of people are more skillful at promoting, branding, diffusing, and imposing them. Social media have intensified this problem. Both socially and politically, today we are driven not by thinkers but by influencers. Thus, Modernity wants us to think that we are driven by reason and post-Modernity that we are manipulated by power through stories.

It is possible, however, that the focus on reason, narrative, and power might have led us to miss something much more fundamental here. When we look at our society, our Church, our forms of political activism, increasingly what is striking is not arguments nor agendas but the growing intransigence of people. There is a lot of anger, fear, shame, and anxiety. It is as if neither reason nor power but these very feelings were the real drivers of our actions, both individually and socially, and that people are just trying to find a relief to them. We pursue our political discourse as if it were still possible to reason people with facts and manipulate them with the help of inspiring stories, but we forget that what drives us as human beings at a fundamental level is what we love and what we hate and that if these potent forces are not taken into account, listened to, and offered a relief, they keep building up a pressure that can burst out of control at any time.

Nobody has a magic solution to these problems, but I would like to point to a few things which have always struck me about the fundamental nature of Christianity. The first is that Jesus never wrote anything. He was a product of Judaism, the religion of the book par excellence; he did teach and talk, but he must not have thought that the key thing about his legacy was the exact wording of his message. He seems to have been quite happy to risk being interpreted, translated, and inevitably misquoted by his disciples. I remember well the joke of an exegete concerning the gigantic effort of some twentieth-century German scholars to reconstruct the *ipsissima verba* of Jesus; that is, the words we can be absolutely, totally, unequivocally sure he pronounced. His view was that the only word which can be traced back to Jesus with certainty, maybe, was "Amen."

Then, the more I studied theology and meditated on Scripture, the more I became amused by a peculiar obsession, almost a pathology, of some forms of Catholicism (both Roman and Anglican) for the words of consecration during the Eucharistic prayer. At what precise instant does the bread and wine become the body and blood of Christ? Classically, this answer has been: in the precise instant in which the priest pronounces the words "This is my body," which are often staged quite dramatically, with genuflections, ostensions, and the ringing of bells. I am not against this, of course. I grew up with it and am emotionally attached to these practices, so I would miss them if they were abolished. And yet, is it not odd that during the Last Supper Jesus should not have asked his disciples to "Say this in memory of me," but to "Do this in memory of me"?

What makes him present among us is the act of gathering in his name, of becoming one body through thanksgiving and through feeding together on the one bread of Christ's own body.

The main point here is that Christianity gets something basic and primary about human nature and community which our Modern and Post-Modern mindsets miss spectacularly. Before being rational and linguistic beings, we are bodies, permeable and responsive to our environment, sensing and reacting to an infinity of stimuli, alternatively excited, startled, interested or afraid, disgusted, distressed, enraged. These feelings, these affects, are not impervious to reason and language, of course. The aim of education is learning to recognize, control, espouse, and assuage them as well as we can.

However, as already Thomas Aquinas (d. 1274) acknowledged in the Middle Ages, these feelings are intractable or highly unpredictable agencies, and the only effective way of dealing with them is negotiating. Rather than to reason and language, these feelings (or passions, or affects) respond to purely physical activities: stress is calmed by a walk, anger by breathing deeply, fear by the reassuring bodily proximity of other people. It seems to me that one of the reasons Christianity is not first of all about precise wording, nor even stories (however important these elements obviously are), is that it knows better.

The fundamental thing that gave shape to Christianity was and still is the dominical bodily gathering around a table to eat and drink in remembrance of Jesus – with all this implies: moving our body somewhere, gathering together to sit, stand, kneel, sing, eat, drink and, why not, play with vestments, candles, smells, bells – playing, after all, is the first social activity through which we learn to interact with others.

This reminds me of something I saw during a walk in one of Beijing's immense parks a few years ago. Every morning, thousands of people gather spontaneously in huge groups to perform synchronized activities: gymnastic, breathing exercises, choreographed movements.

Nothing more than this experience taught me how liturgy builds genuine political communities. Not first of all on the basis of individual rights, universal benefits, affirmative action, political correctness, and identity politics. Nor even primarily trying to establish a consensus on "common objects of love"; that is, on common good, however valuable this would certainly prove to be.

Rather, liturgy provides a space that shapes us as a community by taking seriously our senses, our passions, our affects, and our feelings through giving full hospitality to our bodies – liturgy, in the end, is a place more akin to dance floors and playgrounds than to debating chambers.

So, let us call to mind Maurice Ravel's *Boléro* for a moment and remember the initial motive which is constantly repeated throughout the piece below the variations and amplifications of the melody. In music, it is called an *ostinato* (from the Italian word for "stubborn").

Now, we can say that starting from the day before Jesus died to today, doing this—the Sunday Mass—in memory of Jesus has been the *ostinato* of everything else Christians have sung through their lives and their faith. And the Eucharist's extraordinary community-building power lies in the centrality it grants to bodies, senses, affections, and imagination.

This *ostinato* of the Eucharist is the focal point of Christian tradition. All the other identifying aspects of the Church converge in it, namely ordained ministry, preaching, and baptism. These are the elements that give a recognizable, stable, regular social and institutional structure to the Christian community. As we know, the first thing Jesus did right at the beginning of his public ministry was to choose a number of disciples with no qualifications, no institutional links to the Jewish religious establishment, no particular skills as communicators. They did not have to do anything other than stay with him, share his life, listen to his teaching, ask silly questions and try not to quarrel with each other too much. This sounds like a caricature, but it is not. When the book of Acts specifies the qualities that the person who had to replace Judas should possess, they name only one: to have been part of the group of the disciples "during all the time that the Lord Jesus went in and out among us, beginning from the baptism of John until the day when he was taken up from us" (Acts 1:21-22).

Of course, during this time the disciples also heard Jesus' teachings to the crowds, listened to him when he was explaining the Scriptures to them – so there was an element of learning in this relationship. But the aspect that mattered most was being close to him long enough to reach the kind of acquaintance that only comes with time, in a way not too dissimilar to what we saw in Steve Jobs' care to hand over Apple to someone who had lived and worked with him over many years and therefore had become acquainted not only with his ideas, but especially with his style, priorities, and all the other aspects of a person's vision that cannot be easily grasped through ideas or translated into codifiable behaviors. And if one is to believe what people have said about Steve Jobs' propensity to lash out, this kind of sustained life-sharing must have included a great deal of confrontation.

Had I been one of the apostles the day Jesus was about to ascend to heaven and told them to go and make disciples of all nations teaching them all he had taught them (Mt 28:28-30), I would have panicked: "But I didn't take any notes when you were teaching!! You should have warned us beforehand that you expected this from us – we would have started to write things down"! They quickly understood, however, that there was nothing to worry about: to accomplish the task they had been given, they only had to trust that which they had become, thanks to this sustained acquaintance with Jesus. Indeed, Jesus himself had assured them that when the moment came to give witness to him, they should not worry about what to say but trust the answer welling up from within (cf. Mt 10:19).

Jesus' disciples, on their turn, did the same when their time came to leave this world: they chose some "servants" (that is, deacons), some elders (that is, "priests") and some overseers (that is, "bishops") following exactly the same principles: these had to be people who could be trusted because of what they had become through the breaking of the bread in remembrance of Jesus, through listening to stories about Jesus, and through experiencing forgiveness and loving care in the Christian community.

Theology, therefore, understands tradition, continuity, and regularity in a way which resembles what happens in secular institutions and could be summed up in the *ostinato* of leadership, culture, and rituals. If anything of Jesus' vision and genius has managed to trickle down to us, at least partly, we owe it to this *ostinato*. Often, and rightly, we complain about the shortcomings of leadership, the rigidity of the culture and the repetitiveness of the rituals that sustain Christian tradition.

Already on the basis of what we have seen so far, however, we can ask ourselves how much of this inadequacy of Christian tradition results from our own lack of commitment. Again, Jesus' instructions during the Last Supper were clear: it is not about what we say but about what we do, that is, how present we are with our bodies, how much we invest in relationships within our community, how loyal and caring we are for each other. In one word, it is all about our own *ostinato*, that is, the stubbornness of our own commitment, our own determination to be there, for God, for each other, and for the world.

"Let us mind the same thing" (Phil. 3:16): Monastic Inspiration for Parish Life

Rev. Dr. Alexis Torrance

In the previous paper, we sketched the rudiments of the early history of the monastic movement in the East, paying most attention to the way in which it understood itself as an application of the Gospel, a harnessing in particular of the ascetic impulse of the New Testament. We dwelt on the rationale of the monks for their way of life and how it was seen as culminating not in isolation but in loving communion with God and ardent intercession for the world. We also looked at the tension that arose early on between monasticism and the wider Church, and how both monks themselves and the Church institution sought to make sure that monasticism was never divorced from, or considered a superior alternative to, life in the Church. The accent fell on the Apostle Paul's question "Is Christ divided?," emphasizing that monastic life must be anchored in Christ and so find its proper place and function within Christ's saving Body of the Church, not apart from it or in conflict with it. This ideal of insisting on the harmony between the different functions within the Body has not always been perfectly upheld, but it is fundamental to Christian theology. Monasticism and married life are different. But difference is not the same as contradiction. We should celebrate this difference rather than act suspiciously or judgmentally when confronted with it. Christ cannot be divided.

So if the main aim of my first paper was to make the case that monasticism belongs organically to the undivided Body of Christ, despite its distinctiveness and difference, in this paper the emphasis will be placed on the underlining *unity* that embraces all forms of Christian life, whether monastic or lay, and thus on our ability not simply to accept, honor, or celebrate the monastic path from a distance but to actively *learn from and be nourished by it* within the everyday life of the parish. The ground of this unity between all forms of Christian life is, of course, our Lord Jesus Christ himself, God made flesh for the salvation of all. The Son of God becomes the Son of Man in order to raise us to himself, to grant us to share, by the coming of the Holy Spirit, in his divine sonship of the Immortal Father, granting us adoption as true children of the Most High. This unfathomable mystery makes all human efforts and striving pale to oblivion before its power and might, and in this way it serves to humble all of us, monastic or lay, and to remind us that we are all servants of a common Master and Redeemer, that none of us can save ourselves. As well as this overarching theological view of what binds all Christian forms of life together, however, there is another, related, and in a sense more concrete "equalizer" in Christianity. This great equalizer is none other than the commandments of Christ. Many differences, even "inequalities" of sorts, persist in human life, and Christian life is not immune from them. The commandments of Christ, however, remain the same for everybody. They act as not only the great equalizer but also the great unifier within Christianity, regardless of an individual member's path in life: "by this shall all know that you are my disciples, if you have love for one another" (John 13:35). The new commandment of love "unto the end" is the best known and really the *definitive* commandment of the Gospel. Yet the love that Christ commands of us is not always easy to comprehend. There is a temptation especially in recent decades to cheapen, reduce, or even replace the meaning of love as Christ commands it, eliding it with the simple pursuit of our desires, or the celebration of those who pursue theirs. Such counterfeit love is really only a short-lived emotional or psychological satisfaction that cannot stomach the sight of the Cross, let alone revere it, take it up, and bear it. But the love commanded of Christians is precisely a crucified love, a love "that suffereth long and is kind," as Paul says, that "envieth not," that "vaunteth not itself," that "is not puffed up" (1 Cor. 13:4). All these qualifiers are themselves commandments too, commandments to endure, to not be envious but have "an eye single and full of light," to humble ourselves, and so on. We learn about love and its content, in other words, from the practice of all the commandments.[1]

Before we continue and connect this discussion to the relationship between monastic theology and parish life, we should pause over the meaning of this word "commandment," which is an ugly word in the minds of many Christians. Does it not conjure up the specter of legalism, not to say pharisaism? Or represent the reduction of the Christian message to a rulebook, a legal code that is fundamentally opposed to the liberating message of the Gospel? Are we not under grace, rather than the law? Certainly, if by law we mean specific Old Testament prescriptions, say, regarding clean and unclean foods, then Christians understand the Gospel to be a far cry from that. But the commandments of Christ are not a kind of external code that may have had a positive role for a given time and context (like the dietary laws of the Old Testament), but can now be jettisoned in the name of "grace." The reverence in the Old Testament for the divine law is, like everything else in the Old Testament, something that is *fulfilled* in Christ rather than destroyed by his coming. The fulfillment of this law, the revelation of its deeper meaning, is put on full display, for example, in Christ's Sermon on the Mount: "you have heard it said . . . *but I say unto you.*" In each case, Christ takes a commandment of the Law and *intensifies* it. Not just "do not commit adultery" but do not even accept the *thought* of

---

[1] I try to discuss some themes related to this sentiment in modern Orthodox theology in Alexis Torrance, "The Category of 'Ethical Apophaticism' in Modern Orthodox Theology," *International Journal of Systematic Theology* 23:1 (2021): 41-56.

it, not just "love thy neighbor, hate thine enemy" but *love your enemies.*" This is what the fulfillment of the law looks like, and he is himself, of course, its embodiment. This is an extremely important point. The commandments are not just a revelation of how God wants us to behave; they are a revelation of *how God himself is.* The commandments of Christ reveal something about the divine life itself. This is also why they are so unapologetically demanding, so lofty and exalted. Christ has come and traced within our own human nature the likeness of his divine life, and has summoned us to acquire this very same life in him: to "be perfect, as your heavenly Father is perfect" (Matt. 5:48). No one is exempt from this call. Yet, simultaneously, no one can attain it by their individual efforts. The poet George MacDonald (d. 1905) famously penned the line, "I am a beast until I love as God doth love."[2] Yet how can we love with a love that is not ours, a love that is not of this world? It must be given: "Herein is love, not that we loved God, but that he loved us" (1 John 4:10). The Son of God is our access to the Father's love by the descent of the Holy Spirit. And yet God wills that all be saved, that all receive this love, that all keep Christ's commandments and thereby inherit the divine life to which these commandments testify.

If we can define the common call shared by every Christian, whatever their walk of life, as the reception and living out of divine love, then we must think about what it is that thwarts us in receiving and living out such love. It

---

[2] George MacDonald, *Diary of an Old Soul* (14 January).

may be painful for us to hear, but it is also rather simple. Christ himself tells us what thwarts us. It is ourselves: "if anyone will come after me, let him *deny himself*, and take up his cross daily, and follow me" (Luke 9:23; cf. Matt. 16:24; Mark 8:34). We ourselves get in the way. We mount our egos on high, and so chase away divine love. We exchange the love of God for the love of ourselves, the will of God for self-will, and so we continue the ancestral sin in our own lives. This is why Christ's commandment of love can take the harshest tone at times, and even be formulated as a commandment of hate: "If anyone comes to me, and hates not his father, and mother, and wife, and children, and brethren, and sisters, yea, and his own life also, he cannot be my disciple" (Luke 14:26). A modern Orthodox monk, Sophrony the Athonite (d. 1993), spoke of this paradox in terms of "love to the point of self-hatred."[3] The love of God cannot be compared to any other love. Of course, the hatred of self mentioned by Christ is not to be confused with a psychological malady. The Gospel cannot be reduced to psychological categories. It is rather a firm jolt that makes us aware that "we are not our own, but we are bought with a price" (cf. 1 Cor. 6:19–20), that the infinite value of each of us is not measured by some quality or characteristic that we might be tempted to love about ourselves: it is measured by the Cross. It is a reminder, in other words, to place all our love, all our identity, in Jesus Christ. This is the kind of

---

[3] Archimandrite Sophrony, *We Shall See Him As He Is* (Tolleshunt Knights, UK: Patriarchal Stavropegic Monastery of Saint John the Baptist, 2002), 141-149.

hatred for ourselves that Christ is talking about: a seeking first, with all our being, of the kingdom of God and his righteousness (cf. Matt. 6:33).

This brings us, then, to monasticism and its relevance for all Christians. On this path of attempting to keep Christ's commandments with all one's heart, all one's mind, all one's body, and all one's soul, we witness not only the quest common to all Christians of abandoning the unnatural and sinful passions and habits that close us off from divine love, but even all the attachments to what is natural and not in itself blameworthy (family, relatives, married life, children), for the sake once again of divine love. If the latter is done for reasons that are contrary to divine love, out of contempt for what is natural, for instance, or arrogant self-righteousness, then it is not a legitimate manifestation of the Christian ascetic impulse. But if it is driven by divine love, by a thirst to more perfectly love God and neighbor after the likeness of Christ (as we see in the lives of the monastic saints all down the centuries), then it holds out crucial lessons for all of us. This is because, as I have said, the Christian life is *one* life, centered on our Lord, and thus those who may have been led farther up and farther into it than most can serve as guides and signposts to the rest. "Though ye have ten thousand instructors in Christ, yet have ye not many fathers, for in Christ Jesus I have begotten you through the Gospel" (1 Cor. 4:15). This ability to be a father or mother in Christ is not, of course, the prerogative of monks or nuns in the Church, but it is nonetheless natural to find a connection, given the intensity of the monastic attempt to live in Christ-likeness.

To draw out some of these potential lessons from the desert but for the city, as it were, I would like to concentrate on one very powerful way in which early monasticism (and Eastern monasticism ever since) understood its attempt to acquire divine love. As we have already said, the goal of Christian life cannot be acquired by our own efforts. The content of that goal is the divine life itself, not made by the work of our hands. Yet we simultaneously realize how far and tragically short we fall of the goal, and we yearn for the gap to be overcome, for the wall of separation to be torn down between us and our Maker. Of course, this distance is overcome in the Incarnation, and the wall of separation is definitively torn down in the person, and by the work, of Christ. But this must also translate into our own lives. The healing of humanity in Christ needs to be manifest in the healing of you and me. What is missing? God has accomplished it all for us on the Cross, through the Resurrection, the Ascension, the sending of the Holy Spirit, the establishment of the Church and her saving sacraments, especially of Baptism and the Eucharist. But Orthodox Christianity has always insisted, and not without scriptural warrant, that all these things must be knit together with our willingness, our free assent to "yield our members as servants to righteousness unto holiness" (cf. Rom. 6:19). What does it mean to "yield" to God's work in us? It means, at root, to enact in our lives the prayer "Thy will be done."

This is connected to the notion of self-denial that I touched on earlier: *not my will, but thine, be done.* God does not compel or force us to be saved. He knocks persistently on the door of our heart, but he does not batter it down. So what is the particularly potent monastic way of looking at the phenomenon of consciously acquiring, in our hearts, our minds, our souls, and even our bodies, the free gift of divine love in Christ? It is to look at the whole of Christian life through the lens of *repentance*.[4]

Repentance is both a rather neglected but also misunderstood concept in contemporary Christian discourse. As with the idea of the commandments of Christ, it tends to be viewed in a rather narrow, constricted, not to say suffocating manner. Yet, like the commandments in general, repentance is anything but. It is itself, of course, one of Christ's commandments, and a key one at that. The summons to repentance inaugurates Christ's whole public ministry: "From that time Jesus began to preach, and to say, Repent: for the kingdom of heaven is at hand" (Matt. 4:17). The Greek imperative verb here is μετανοεῖτε, which means "keep repenting." The word for repentance, μετάνοια, can be broken down to the terms *meta* (like in the words *meta*physics or *meta*phor) and *nous* (which roughly corresponds to mind or intellect). In other words, repentance means a radical change of mind, of inner orientation, in this case for the sake of the kingdom of heaven. The significance

---

[4] This is the subject of my monograph *Repentance in Late Antiquity: Eastern Asceticism and the Framing of the Christian Life, ca. 400–650* (Oxford: Oxford University Press, 2013).

of this being Christ's opening commandment was not lost on early Christians. Mark the Monk (5th c.), whom we met in the last paper on the importance of baptism, meditates on this significance thus:

> Our Lord Jesus Christ, the power and wisdom of God, foreseeing for the salvation of all what he knew was worthy of God, decreed the law of liberty by means of various teachings, and to all set a single goal (ἕνα σκοπὸν), saying, "Repent," so that we might understand by this that all the diversity of the commandments is summed up by one word: repentance.[5]

If, then, the commandments in general unite all Christians, monastic or lay, around a common and shared task, the commandment of repentance has the added quality, according to Mark, of neatly capturing the essence of all those various commandments in one go. To live as a Christian, according to Mark, is to repent. Mark was one of many early monastic writers to frame all of Christian life around this term, to produce a kind of "science of repentance" that tried to make sense both of the specific monastic path, but at the same time of all Christian striving. This idea may at first blush sound somber, dark, or excessively negative, so we must try to unpack the meaning of repentance to help reveal the positive and light-bearing message it contains.

We tend to think of repentance as simply a form of regret, a sorrow for sin, a turning *away from* something.

---

[5] Mark the Monk, *On Repentance* 1.1–7 (SC 445:214); my translation. Unless otherwise noted, all translations are my own.

Repentance includes all these things, of course, but its basis is not in fact grounded in them. Jesus does not say "repent because of your sin" but "repent *because of the kingdom.*" He places the bearings of repentance in his kingdom, ultimately orienting repentance towards *himself.* From the beginning, repentance is understood in the gospels as not just a turn *away* from something, then, but *towards* something, or rather *towards Someone.* This does not, importantly, *exclude* the real need for change, for turning away from our destructive passions and habits, but such change is *already included* in the positive re-orientation of the human being towards Christ and his kingdom. The positive takes precedence in this understanding of repentance. We repent not simply because we want to stop sinning but because we want to commune with God, because we want to be united to Christ, to be joint-heirs with him. When we begin to see repentance from this perspective, we can perhaps start to understand why early monasticism found it so congenial for thinking about their way of life (and Christian life as a whole). If the measure of repentance is not just concerned with abandoning this or that sin or destructive passion, but with wholly acquiring "the mind of Christ" (cf. 1 Cor. 2:16), straining to be conformed to "the measure of the stature of his fullness" (cf. Eph. 4:13), then it becomes a task and commandment that has no end on earth. If we cannot claim to truly be as Christ is, then our repentance is incomplete, and if our repentance is incomplete, then we automatically forfeit any right to boast of this or that ascetic achievement or righteous deed. Our thirst for complete union with Christ leads us, like Paul, to "count all things but loss for the excellency of the knowledge of Christ Jesus my Lord . . . forgetting those things which are behind, and reaching forth unto those things which are before" (Philippians 3:8, 13). This is the essence of repentance. But to elaborate on this, I would like to draw on some of the work I did in my first book, which is devoted to the theme of repentance in early Greek monastic literature. There I found that the early monks spoke about repentance in three distinct but interrelated ways. This threefold approach to repentance might help us not only to understand monastic theology better but also to see the relevance of this theology for all Christians.

Initial Repentance

The first way of approaching repentance is to see it as an entry-point, a beginning or new beginning. We could call this "initial" repentance. It can be linked to the prickings of conscience, and is manifest, for instance, in the parable of the Prodigal Son, who, it says "came to himself." It is an awakening, an inner realization that we are far from our Father's house, that we have squandered the many gifts and blessings given to us, that we must "arise and go to my Father and say: Father, I have sinned against heaven and before thee; make me as one of thy hired servants" (Luke 15:18-19). This initial repentance does not, however, only take this form of self-realization and confession. It has a sacramental form too. Initial repentance is first and foremost fulfilled through none other than Christian baptism. The preaching of the Apostles after Pentecost, if you recall, made this connection clear: "repent and be baptized" (Acts 2:38). Repentance is powerless and not worthy of the name if it remains only a self-realization of inadequacy, or a self-loathing that does not orient itself towards putting on Christ. Once Christ has been irrevocably put on, however, through baptism, does this signal the end of repentance? A minority of rigorists in the early Church basically thought so. Thus Tertullian (d. ca. 220) left the Church in the early third century for the heresy of the Montanists in part because he felt the Church was not rigorous enough on the matter of repentance. And Novatian (d. 258), a presbyter in Rome, began a schismatic movement also in the third century predicated on the need for rigor and tight controls on the possibility of repentance after baptism. But these, I have argued, are anomalies within the tradition. One of the key texts used by the rigorists was Hebrews 6:5-6, in which it is said that in the case of certain offenders it was impossible, "if they shall fall away, to renew them again unto repentance." In reaction to this reading of the text, some such as Mark the Monk, turned this interpretation on its head. The text does not say, he explains, that repentance is not possible after baptism, but rather that a second "renewal," namely a second baptism, is inadmissible. In fact, baptism is being defined here, says Mark, as a renewal *into* repentance (*eis metanoian*), not a leaving aside of repentance. Repentance, on this reading, becomes not just something that precedes baptism and is then set aside, but something that really only *begins in earnest* with baptism. We initially repent for the sake of baptism, but we are also baptized *for the sake of repentance.* This may seem counter-intuitive, but it becomes less so when we remember that repentance is about our real and conscious assimilation to Christ. Baptism enacts that assimilation in a hidden or mystical way in Mark's theology, but it must be manifested *actively* through the keeping of the commandments, the supreme commandment being that of repentance.

So initial repentance cannot be the whole story on this monastic reading. It does, however, figure prominently, and we can associate it not only with pre-baptismal repentance, but with every new beginning in our spiritual life, every time we "come to ourselves" and seek to return to the Father. This too has a sacramental expression, more prominent of course in the Orthodox tradition than in Protestantism, namely confession. Confession has been a much-debated phenomenon in Western Christianity since the time of the Reformation, and certainly we can create problems if we think of repentance as *only* being about the exposure of one's sins to God in the presence of a priest. But it is clear that this was certainly *part* of what repentance could mean to early Christians. The awe-inspiring gift of the binding and loosing of sins by the Holy Spirit, that was imparted to Christ's apostles is not simply a theoretical gift imparted impersonally to the Church as a whole. There is nothing impersonal in the Church of Christ. It is imparted to *specific persons*, and it is exercised *for specific persons*. The dangers of creating a bureaucratic industry out of this kind of repentance is amply critiqued by the early Reformers. In fact, the first of Luther's *Ninety-Five Theses* takes aim at this distortion. But the distortions of late medieval Roman Catholicism do not justify the wholesale rejection of the real gift of grace to bind and loose given to the Church. In the East, the development of the practice of confession does not take on the character of an institutional bureaucracy, where for instance indulgences might be issued, functionally speaking, in exchange for donations. It reflects more the monastic practice of laying bare one's soul to a spiritual guide in the faith. In monasticism, this takes on a rather intense and intricate character, where not only one's particular sins, but even one's thoughts, are set out, sometimes on a daily basis, and the spiritual father guides the monk accordingly. The concern with thoughts (*logismoi*) in one's spiritual life is extremely important in the monastic tradition. It stems from Scripture's injunction to "keep thy heart with all diligence" (Prov. 4:23) and Christ's warning that it is "out of the heart" that evil thoughts, murders, adulteries, fornications, thefts, false witness, and blasphemies proceed into the world (cf. Matt. 15:19). Caring about the contents of the "treasure of our heart" (cf. Luke 6:45) forms a vital task of the Christian, and the monastic tradition could be said to specialize in this art. This art has as its goal "bringing into captivity every thought to the obedience of Christ" (2 Cor. 10:5). It is, as such, yet another expression of repentance. It would be hard, however, to limit this endeavor to simply an "initial" kind of repentance, a simple beginning or new beginning. Thus, we find in monastic literature the idea that repentance is not just about a beginning or first step but is an ongoing and living expression of all of Christian existence. We can term this *lived* or *existential* repentance.

Existential Repentance

To get to grips with this idea of existential repentance and its possible relevance for everyday Christian life, we can continue with the thought of Mark the Monk. He argues that "repentance, in my opinion, is neither limited to times or actions, but it is practiced in proportion with the commandments of Christ."[6] Repentance is thus not simply a commandment, but the *mode* through which all the other commandments are fulfilled. It serves not just as a springboard to Christian life; it *gives shape* to what it means to live as a Christian, an ethos that conditions the Christian's whole outlook. The continual living out of repentance occurs, however, not through cultivating a guilty conscience or obsessing over trying to be sad all the time. It occurs naturally via the keeping of the other commandments. Mark singles out three general commandments, subsidiary to repentance, that he feels are especially important: the

---

[6] Mark the Monk, *On repentance* 6.25–27 (SC 445:232).

rejection of thoughts (a term employed by Paul, sometimes translated "casting down imaginations"); unceasing prayer; and the patient endurance of whatever comes our way. Each of these commandments is a general commandment insofar as it contains many others.

Thus, through attentiveness to our thoughts and the struggle to conform them to Christ, we nip in the bud the development of all sorts of potentially destructive passions and ideas. We work the earth of our heart, in other words, in order to welcome the gentle rain of divine grace, co-laboring for our spiritual growth. Or, to use another image employed by Mark and other monastic fathers, we perform the inner liturgy on the altar of our hearts, offering to God the first-fruits of our minds, that is, the thoughts that preoccupy us. We sacrifice them before him, asking for the descent of the fire of his grace upon this sacrifice, to consume what must be consumed, and to transfigure what remains for our spiritual nourishment. This process of the purification of thoughts, then, entails the second general commandment of unceasing prayer.

As with the first general commandment regarding thoughts, prayer is by no means limited to monastic life. It is sometimes said that Christianity is a religion of *action*. This is occasionally meant as a snub to the more contemplative expressions of Christian life, as though no one had ever read what Christ said to Mary and Martha about the one thing needful. Of course, Christianity *is* a religion of action. What we must realize, however, is that *prayer is an action* and that it is, in fact, the most creative and potent activity available to human beings. This is not to denigrate other Christian activity (Mary and Martha, after all, are both considered saints in the Christian tradition). It is simply to give prayer its due. The Byzantine monastic tradition calls prayer "the art of arts and the science of sciences" in an effort to show how it is not to be seen as an *alternative* to action or engagement, but *as the highest form of it*. Prayer signifies both communication and also *communion* with God. It also signifies communion, by grace, with our neighbor. Prayer is a wonder-working quality that we all have access to, and which we all have a responsibility to undertake. Not, it is true, in a Pharisaical manner, for self-display, nor for the sake of things contrary to the divine will. Mark has in mind the prayer begotten of a heart aflame with the desire for God, or even just a heart that *wishes* to be aflame with this desire.

One prayer that became extremely important in Byzantine monastic circles and is now emphasized throughout the Orthodox world and beyond is the so-called Jesus Prayer, which runs with variations like this: "Lord Jesus Christ, Son of God, have mercy upon me, a sinner [or 'upon us']." The frequent if not unceasing repetition of this prayer has become a hallmark of Orthodox spirituality. It is an attempt to put into practice the command of unceasing prayer, and notice that it is formulated both using scriptural language as well as a focus on none other than *repentance*. It is a prayer of repentance, an invocation of the saving name of Jesus Christ, asking him to dwell within our hearts, to pour his mercy upon us, to make us, though sinners, into his brethren, adopted children of the Father. There is an Orthodox monastery in England that I have visited since I was a boy. They place a strong emphasis on the practice of the Jesus Prayer and even substitute the invocation of the Jesus Prayer in a communal setting in place of many of the weekday services. Once, a Roman Catholic priest was visiting the monastery and asked the monastery's founder, "Why is it that you repeat this prayer so often? Does it not get boring or tiresome?" The priest replied, "We repeat it so much because we are slow to understand it. But when we have understood it, we do not want to abandon it." The beauty of this short prayer is that it can accompany us in any circumstance. Whatever our job, our commitments, our responsibilities, we can always find a way to sneak this prayer into our daily lives, to catch ourselves and re-orient our hearts and minds towards the one thing needful, our Lord himself. If we slowly but surely punctuate our lives ever more frequently with this prayer (and other prayers, too, of course), then perhaps we will begin to see the grace of healing ever more clearly at work within us.

Together with rejection of thoughts and unceasing prayer, Mark highlights endurance as a third general means of continuously keeping the commandment to repent. By endurance, he does not mean just to "grin and bear" whatever happens to you. Outward endurance is only part of the story. Our Lord told us that "in patience you will gain your souls" (Luke 21:19) and "he that endureth to the end shall be saved" (Matt. 10:22). The patience meant here is a resoluteness not only in our outward demeanor, but in our whole being: mind, heart, soul, and body. It is about fixing our gaze on Christ through both the blessings and the trials that come our way, seeing trials themselves as blessings. But this resoluteness and fixing of the gaze is not the same as an unfeeling, stoic persistence. As a form of repentance, patience is not motivated by endurance for endurance's sake, but rather for the sake of the kingdom. As we read concerning the endurance of Christ, "who for the joy that was set before him endured the cross, despising the shame" (Heb. 12:2), the motivation is *the joy of Christ's kingdom*. And that joy animates all Christian patience or endurance. The Christian not only grins and bears it when afflictions or tribulations arise outside one's control but endures them gladly, even with thanksgiving. Here we encounter a paradox in the early monastic understanding of repentance, namely that our repentance can be expressed, and is perhaps best expressed, through the act of giving thanks to God for all that comes our way, whether good or ill. This principle is summarized nicely in the sixth-century letters of Barsanuphius of Gaza (d. 540): "thanksgiving intercedes before God for our weaknesses."[7] Through thanksgiving (*eucharistia* in Greek) we take up the Eucharistic ethos that is central to the Christian Gospel. Thanksgiving is so

---

[7] Barsanuphius and John, *Letter* 214.17–18 (SC 427.666). Cf. Letters 77, 92, 123 for a repetition of the same idea in similar terms.

powerful, especially when we give thanks in tribulations and afflictions, because we thereby associate ourselves with the one who endured like a lamb all pain and suffering on our behalf. And like the Jesus Prayer, thanksgiving is always and everywhere available to us. What is stopping us from crying out from the depths: "Glory be unto thee, O Christ our God and our hope, glory be unto thee! Though I am unworthy, thou dost wish to heal and save even the likes of me. Unto thee be glory for ever and ever!" The power of thanksgiving as a form of repentance is eloquently expressed, incidentally, in one of the sayings of the desert fathers. It runs like this:

> Two monks, who were attacked by lust, abandoned the monastery and took to themselves women. Afterwards they said to each other: 'What have we gained that we have ceased to live like angels, and have come to this impurity, and later will come to fire and torment? Let us go back to the desert, and repent for our fault.' And they came to the desert, and asked the fathers to accept them, and confessed what they had done. And the elders shut them up for a whole year, and gave them each an equal measure of bread and water. Now they were alike in appearance. And at the end of the year, they came out. And the fathers saw that one looked pale and melancholy, the other looked strong and bright. And they were astonished, for each had had the same quantity of food and drink. And they asked the man who was sad and troubled: 'What were you doing with your thoughts in that cell?' And he said: 'I was turning over in my mind the punishment I shall incur for the evil I have done, and I was so afraid that my bones cleaved to my flesh.' And they asked the other: 'What were you thinking about in your cell?' And he said: 'I was thanking God that he

had delivered me from the impurity of this world and the punishment of the next, and has called me back to live here like the angels: and as I continually thought upon God, I was made glad.' And the old men said: 'The repentance of both men is equal before God.'[8]

From this little story we glean not only something about the power of repentance in the minds of the early monks, but specifically of thanksgiving as a positive and healthy tool of reconciliation with God.

Christ-like Repentance

I have spoken of repentance as being discussed in three distinct yet overlapping ways in the early monastic tradition. So far we have looked at initial repentance and existential or lived repentance. There is one more, and I want to conclude my talk with it. I have said that the commandments of Christ are not a legal code but revelations of the divine life and invitations to assimilate that life in the Church. I have also discussed how repentance can be seen as an all-encompassing commandment, an interpretive key, as it were, for making sense of the other commandments (even, I would argue, the chief commandment of love). This is because repentance means, at root, orienting oneself towards Christ and away from everything contrary to Christ. But we might stop to ask: if the commandments reveal the divine life, and if repentance is a commandment,

---

[8] *Apophthegmata Patrum* (anonymous collection) N 186 (SC 387:278–80).

then how can repentance be said to reveal anything about the divine life? Surely Christ did not need repentance, since he was without sin. So how do we connect these points? The answer lies in this third approach to repentance in monastic literature, which I term *Christ-like repentance.* What does this mean?

Well, in discussing repentance as an ongoing and continual process (what I have called *existential* repentance), the early monks thought through what the implications are of saying that the goal of repentance is union with Christ, but that repentance also has no limit or end on earth. Does this just mean that we are never really united to Christ in this life? That could be one interpretation, although the monks were insistent on the possibility of real and fruitful communion with Christ here and now. This is where the third approach to repentance comes in. Christ himself needed no repentance, and yet his whole work of salvation could nonetheless be seen as an act of repentance: repenting on behalf of all and for all. Our old friend Mark the Monk discusses this idea in a question-and-answer format:

> 'Tell me, those who fall into debt because of their own borrowing, are they alone debtors or are their guarantors also?' The subordinate answered saying: 'their guarantors also of course.' The old man went on: 'Know it well that in becoming our guarantor, Christ constituted himself a debtor according to the Holy Scriptures: 'the lamb of God who takes away the sin of the world' (Jn 1.29), 'the one who became a curse for us' (Gal 3.3), 'the one who took upon himself the death of all and died on behalf of all' (cf. 2 Cor

5.14).[9]

Jesus Christ, in other words, *does* repent, but just not for himself. He has no need of repentance in the sense of a personal "re-orientation of mind," but in a deeper, ontological sense, in his humanity, and specifically through his death on the Cross, he "repents" for all humanity, by tearing down the wall of enmity between us and God, abolishing sin and the law of sin, "blotting out the handwriting of ordinances that was against us, which was contrary to us, and took it out of the way, nailing it to his cross" (Col. 2:14).[10] This "repentance" of Christ is an expression of the divine life, insofar as it manifests the love of God, the *way God is* in relation to his creatures. When this is transferred to our own repentance by the monastic writers, we encounter something striking, what we might call the concept of Christ-like repentance. Mark the Monk puts it succinctly thus: "the saints are obliged to offer repentance for their neighbor, since without an active love it is impossible to be perfected."[11] The end of repentance really has no end, that is to say, because in the very process of conforming ourselves to Christ, of having one common mind with him, our repentance opens out towards the other. Repentance and intercession coalesce, such that the Christian bears in

---

[9] Mark the Monk, *Dialogue with a lawyer* 15.12–23 (SC 455:70).

[10] For a profound meditation on the idea of Christ's repentance along these lines, see Khaled Anatolios, *Deification through the Cross: An Eastern Christian Theology of Salvation* (Grand Rapids, MI: Eerdmans, 2020).

[11] Mark the Monk, *On repentance* 11.15–17 (SC 445:250).

their heart not just their own brokenness before God, but that of each and all. There is a mystery here, but it is once again not the exclusive preserve of monastic "elites." The monks may sketch out this mystery more clearly than most, but even if only in a small way, this form of repentance is available to all. Paul summons all Christians to something similar when he says, "bear one another's burdens" (Gal. 6:2). It is telling that he even calls this "the law of Christ." Christianity does have a law. It is the life-giving law of the Gospel, of laying down one's life for one's friends. It is the logic of love that puts God and neighbor before oneself, that gladly and ardently intercedes for the healing and salvation of all. This is what it means for Christians "to mind the same thing" (Phil. 3:16). The unity of monastic and lay life is unbreakable insofar as both are bonded and grafted into Christ's Body. Fissures begin to form, and tragic alienation from the Vine follows, only when we forget or neglect the common task of all Christians to serve and love our Lord through the keeping of his commandments. The goal is not to make life in the parish more monastic, nor life in the monastery more like a parish: the goal is, once again, to mind the same thing, to be united in faith, in hope, and in the incorruptible love that truly unites us to God and to one another.